sue kay

jon hird

peter maggs

move

upper-intermediate

coursebook
with CD-ROM

Contents map

Module 3 Places

CD-ROM

Location	• Modules 1–3, Units 1–4
Activities for each unit	• Language activity • Vocabulary activity • Common European Framework linked activity • Language game
Features	• Markbook – helps you to record and update your marks. • Bookmark – helps you to save your favourite activities. • Wordlist – helps you to create your own wordlists. • You can back up, restore and print out your Markbook, Bookmarks and Wordlists. You can also send saved files as emails. • For more information use the Help feature.

In the Coursebook:

three 32-page modules

On the CD-ROM:

48 language activities and games,
a help section and markbook, wordlist and
bookmark features

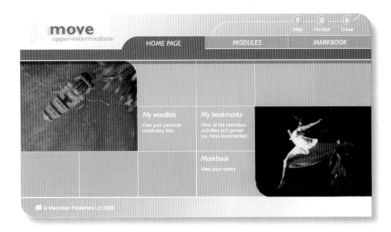

In each module:

four main units

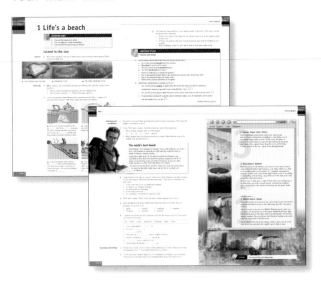

a review unit

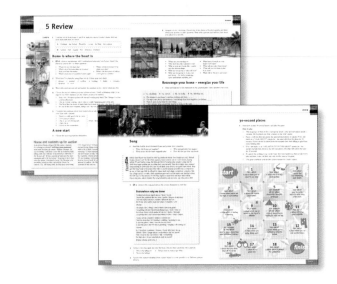

four extra practice pages

five reference pages: grammar,
wordlist and listening scripts

two communication
activity pages

Module 1
People

Unit	Topic	Language study	Vocabulary	Main skills
1 Making an impression pages 2–5	• It's all in the hues that you choose (The colours to wear at an interview) • How much of a go-getter are you? • Don't call us, we'll call you (Things that went wrong in an interview)	• Talking about the past (narrative tenses) • *be supposed to / be meant to / be going to*	• Personal qualities and characteristics	• **Reading:** understanding key information • **Pronunciation:** word stress • **Listening:** understanding gist and identifying key information • **Speaking:** discussing first impressions; responding to a questionnaire; telling an anecdote
2 A shoulder to cry on pages 6–9	• Whatever happened to whatsisname? (Types of friend and changes in friendship) • The word on the street (What women look for in a partner)	• The language of reporting on a survey	• Friendship • Expressions for describing a partner	• **Listening:** identifying main topics and key information; predicting and checking • **Reading:** understanding key information • **Speaking:** discussing friendship and partners; discussing what annoys / fascinates you, etc
3 You're as old as you feel pages 10–13	• The secret of a long life • An old head on young shoulders (The singer Joss Stone)	• Uses of the infinitive	• Age and long life • Different uses of *like*	• **Listening:** identifying main topics and key information • **Reading:** understanding paragraph topics; understanding vocabulary in context • **Speaking:** discussing the ideal age for different activities; visualising speakers from their voice
4 A dream job pages 14–17	• Follow your dreams • I'd love to do that (Dream jobs)	• Real and hypothetical situations	• Feelings • Phrasal verbs • Jobs	• **Reading:** identifying key information; understanding vocabulary in context; summarising • **Listening:** understanding gist and identifying key information • **Speaking:** discussing ambitions and dream jobs • **Writing:** a CV

1 Making an impression

LEARNING AIMS

- Can use structures to talk about the past
- Can discuss personal qualities and first impressions
- Can understand word stress

Lead-in 1 Work in small groups and discuss these questions.

1 What do you usually notice about people when you first meet them?
2 What can this tell you about them?
3 Are your first impressions usually right?

Reading 1 You are going to read an article about the importance of colour in first impressions. Match the pairs of adjectives to the colours you associate them with.

1	fun / entertaining	4	superficial / submissive	7	calm / level-headed
2	deep / spiritual	5	enthusiastic / ambitious	8	dependable / rational
3	creative / artistic	6	dull / boring		

2 ◉ **01** Read the article. Compare your ideas in Ex 1 with what the writer says about colour.

It's all in the hues that you choose

Worrying about what to wear to that all-important interview? First impressions count, but dressing right doesn't just mean looking smart. Forget the actual clothing and think more about colours: the hues that you choose could say more about you than you think to a future employer.

RED suggests assertiveness and energy. People who wear red are enthusiastic, ambitious and single-minded, which makes it a good colour to wear if you want to come across as a go-getter.

PINK conveys fluffy bunny. Avoid wearing this to an interview, as it's a colour that suggests a submissive personality and lack of depth.

YELLOW is for cheerfulness and a good sense of humour. Yellow people are fun-loving and gregarious – ideal for someone who wants to work with others as a team-player or an entertainer, but it could signal to your prospective boss that you're a bit of a clown.

BLUE is for intellect. This colour is associated with efficiency and dependability. It's good for lawyers and accountants who want to convey a rational, conventional image, but too sensible for designers and art teachers.

PURPLE has spiritual connotations. It tells an interviewer that you like to be left on your own to meditate. You're self-sufficient and independent, but people may think you're a bit of a loner.

GREEN stands for balance and tolerance. People who wear green are fair, calm under pressure and unflappable, making them suitable as doctors, lawyers and television presenters.

GREY is boring, so don't wear it. It suggests a lack of personality and self-confidence. Being neither black nor white, it shows a lack of conviction.

ORANGE is for creativity and sensuality. It tells an interviewer that you're open-minded and impulsive, and even a little eccentric. Great for entertainers, artists and writers.

'It's all in the hues that you choose' for The Independent

3 Read the article again. According to the writer, which colours:

1 give a good impression?
2 give a bad impression?
3 may give a mixed impression?

4 Complete the definitions with words and expressions from the text.

1 'A _go-getter_' is someone who is determined to succeed and works hard to achieve this. (paragraph 1)

2 'A _____ - _____' is a person who works well with other people as part of a group. (paragraph 3)

3 'A bit of a _____' describes a person who likes to entertain people by doing or saying funny things. (paragraph 3)

4 'A bit of a _____' describes someone who prefers to be independent and to do things on their own. (paragraph 5)

5 Do you know any people who fit the descriptions in Ex 4? Compare your ideas with a partner.

6 Work with a partner. Describe the style and colour of clothes you would wear to create a good impression in these situations.

1 on a first date
2 meeting a girl / boyfriend's parents for the first time
3 at a job interview

Vocabulary and pronunciation

1 Complete the table. Then check your answers in the text.

	adjective	noun		adjective	noun
1	assertive	_assertiveness_	7	_____	spirituality
2	energetic	_____	8	_____	self-sufficiency
3	_____	enthusiasm	9	_____	independence
4	_____	ambition	10	self-confident	_____
5	efficient	_____	11	creative	_____
6	dependable	_____	12	_____	impulsiveness

2 🔘 **02** Mark the main stress on the words in Ex 1. In which pairs of words does the main stress change? Listen and check.

Example: _energetic_ / _energy_

3 Complete these sentences with the appropriate adjectives or nouns in Ex 1.

1 I have this burning _____ to be number one in everything I do.

2 Even though I'm not religious, I think I'm quite a _____ person.

3 I come from a very artistic family and that's where I get my _____ streak.

4 I'm not positive enough about myself. I wish I had more _____.

5 I don't want to live at home with my parents. I'd rather have less money and more _____.

6 I'm often too _____. I tend to act first and think about it later.

7 I need to be more _____. I usually give in to other people too easily.

8 I'm a very positive person and try to be _____ about everything I do.

4 Do any of the sentences in Ex 3 describe you? Compare your ideas with a partner.

Reading and speaking

1 Complete the questionnaire and calculate your score.

2 Read the analysis on page 29 and compare your answers with a partner.

HOW MUCH OF A

go-getter ARE YOU?

1 What do you never leave home without?
a sunglasses and lip balm
b contact / business cards and diary
c credit card and wallet

2 In your free time
a you like to spend time with your friends
b you like to go shopping c what free time?

3 Your friends are always impressed by your:
a sense of style b leadership skills
c dedication to your work or studies

4 The present you would most like to receive is:
a an electronic organiser b tickets for a concert
c the latest mobile phone

5 Who would you most like to have lunch with?
a Bill Gates b The Pope c Justin Timberlake

6 In the next five years, you hope to:
a travel the world, write a book and get a well-paid job
b make more friends and date more people
c get a good home and a secure job

1 a-4 b-1 c-2   4 a-1 b-3 c-2
2 a-2 b-3 c-0   5 a-0 b-2 c-4
3 a-3 b-0 c-1   6 a-1 b-3 c-2

Don't call us, we'll call you

Listening

1 Work with a partner. Think of all the things that could go wrong in an interview.

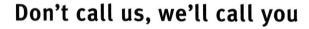

▲ Sarah   ▲ Alice   ▲ Robert

2 🔘 **03** Listen to Sarah, Alice and Robert talking about interviews they attended. Complete these sentences with the correct name.

1 _____ didn't listen to the questions the interviewer asked.

2 _____ didn't show enough respect to one of the interviewers.

3 _____ had had a previous encounter with the interviewer.

3 Listen again. Are these statements true or false? If they are false, say why.

1 At the time of the accident Sarah was talking on her mobile. ☐

2 Sarah felt embarrassed during the interview. ☐

3 Sarah told the interviewer that they had met before. ☐

4 Alice listened to the interview before hers and jotted down the questions and answers. ☐

5 Alice answered the interviewers' questions correctly. ☐

6 Alice's interviewers didn't realise she had been listening through the door. ☐

7 One of Robert's interviewers had been held up in traffic. ☐

8 Robert was chatting away with the woman interviewer when the man arrived. ☐

9 Robert shook the woman's hand but he didn't shake the man's. ☐

LANGUAGE STUDY

Talking about the past

Narrative tenses

1   Look at these extracts from the interview stories. Match the verb forms in **bold** to the uses a–d.

*I (1) **had** this really long interview. It was supposed to be with a man and a woman, but he (2)**'d been held up** in traffic. As we (3) **were chatting** away, he (4) **came** in.*

*I (5) **was waiting** ... outside the interview room and by the time they (6) **called** me, I (7)**'d been waiting** for ages and they (8) **'d already interviewed** three people.*

Past simple	**a** for a completed past event 1 ☐ ☐
Past continuous	**b** for a background activity in progress in the past ☐ ☐
Past perfect simple	**c** for a past event that was completed before another past event ☐ ☐
Past perfect continuous	**d** for a past activity that was in progress before another past event ☐

be supposed to | be meant to | be going to

2   Look at these extracts. Do the verb forms in **bold** refer to something that:
   a   happened as planned?   b   was intended but didn't happen as planned?

   1   *I had this really long interview. It **was supposed to** be with a man and a woman, but he'd been held up.*
   2   *He asked me if we'd met before. I **was going to** tell him, but I just couldn't bring myself to do it.*
   3   *My interview **was meant to** start at nine o'clock, but I was late.*

Grammar reference page 26

3   Complete part 1 of a story about first impressions. Use an appropriate form of the verb.
   I (1 visit) _was visiting_ friends and because I (2 travel) _____ all day, I
   (3 go) _____ to suggest a quiet night in. But my friends (4 already / arrange) _____ to take me out to a restaurant. I (5 just / rave)
   _____ about the meal when the chef (6 come) _____ out of the
   kitchen. My mouth fell open and I realised that I (7 look) _____ at the most
   gorgeous man I (8 ever / see) _____. I (9 hope) _____ that my
   friends wouldn't notice, but it was obvious because every time he came out of the
   kitchen I (10 turn) _____ bright red. I (11 live) _____ quite far
   away at the time, so I got his email address and we (12 start) _____ writing to
   each other. Eventually, we (13 arrange) _____ to meet.

4   🔘 **04** What do you think happened next? Listen and check.

5   Rewrite these sentences using the words in brackets so that the meaning is the same.

   1   I had intended to impress her with my cooking, but it was a disaster. (supposed)
   2   I was sure the exam would be difficult, but it was actually quite easy. (going)
   3   It should have been a big party, but hardly anyone turned up. (meant)
   4   I wanted to tell him how I felt, but I didn't get the chance. (going)
   5   I'd heard our new teacher was really strict, but he's actually very friendly. (supposed)

Speaking   1   Choose one of these topics. Spend a few minutes planning what you are going to say.
   •   a time when your first impressions of somebody were wrong
   •   a time when you made a bad first impression

   2   Work with a partner and tell each other your stories.

CD-ROM   For more activities go to **People Unit 1**

2 A shoulder to cry on

LEARNING AIMS

- Can use the language of reporting on a survey
- Can conduct a survey
- Can discuss friendship

Friendship

Lead-in **1** What do you think are the most important qualities in a friend? Choose three from this list and then compare your ideas with a partner.

A good friend is someone who ...

1	shares your sense of humour	6	you can trust
2	is generous	7	is easy to talk to
3	likes the same music as you	8	is punctual
4	shares your interests	9	doesn't judge you
5	is a good listener	10	can keep a secret

Listening **1** 🔘 **05** Listen to Toby and Jack talking about their friendship. Tick the qualities in Lead-in Ex 1 that they mention.

2 Who do these adjectives describe? Tick one or both boxes. Listen again and check.

		Jack	Toby			Jack	Toby
1	amusing	☐	☐	5	a go-getter	☐	☐
2	left-wing	☐	☐	6	trustworthy	☐	☐
3	right-wing	☐	☐	7	easy-going	☐	☐
4	competitive	☐	☐	8	jealous	☐	☐

3 Work with a partner. Tell each other about a close friend. Talk about how you met and why you became friends.

Reading **1** Which of these statements do you agree with?

1 In a few years you will have lost contact with most of your present friends.
2 People usually have between 30 and 35 friends at any one time.
3 Your best friends are the friends you see most often.
4 Women are more likely than men to keep in regular contact with their friends.
5 As you get older, your group of friends will grow wider.
6 Very few people think that friends are more important than family.

2 🔘 **06** Read the article. Are the statements in Ex 1 true or false?

3 Complete the table with the other categories of friendship: *pruners*, *harvesters* or *gatherers*.

have long-lasting, close friendships

cultivators ↑

maintain frequent ←————————————→ don't maintain
contact   frequent contact

↓

make and drop friends easily

4 Work in small groups and discuss these questions.

1 Which of the four categories in Ex 3 do you think you fit into?
2 Can you think of someone you know who fits into each of the other categories?
3 The article says that 'men are more likely to be *gatherers* or *harvesters*, whereas women dominate the *cultivator* category'. Do you agree with this?

Source: 'Whatever happened to whatsisname?' by Lewis Smith for *The Times*

Whatever happened to
whatsisname?

Count them carefully. You have 33 friends now, yet within a few years you will have lost touch with all but a handful.

You will go through 396 friends in a lifetime but will have only 33 at any one time, says a survey. Of these, only six are close or best friends you can confide in and trust to be there when you need a shoulder to cry on.

According to the survey, best friends are not even the ones that you see most of, but they are the ones you think of more often than any other. The remainder are merely for social occasions and are mainly made up of school or workmates, past and present.

The research identified four categories of friendship.

- **CULTIVATORS**, to whom friends mean a lot, are the most likely to nurture long-term friendships and ensure frequent meetings.

- **PRUNERS** have a tendency towards making friends quickly and dropping them just as fast. They like to be seen in the 'in-crowd' and contact these friends on a regular basis. However, they are ruthless with those they see as uncool, even deleting their names from diaries.

- **HARVESTERS** have a hardcore circle of friends, who they remain close to despite spending long periods making no attempt to meet or even speak to them.

- **GATHERERS** tend to make friends easily and in great numbers, but do little to maintain the relationships and rarely make the effort to keep in touch.

Men are more likely to be gatherers or harvesters, whereas women dominate the cultivator category.

Online technology has created a new kind of companion – the 'silent' friend who people speak to through text messaging and emails. They rarely speak on the phone, and they are even less likely to meet face to face. One in three people admit they have 'silent' friends and say they make contact with them up to four times a day.

The number of people considered to be friends falls steadily as age rises. 'The fact that so many companions get left in the past shows the differences in the levels of friendships,' said Dr Papadopoulos, a psychologist at London University. 'Clearly there are some people we will turn to when things are really bad or really good,' she added. 'Others, those more easily left behind, are social friends, people we enjoy being with but who don't give us the spiritual support we get from deeper friendships.'

Despite the drop-out rate of friends, six out of ten people claimed they value their friendships more than money, successful careers or even family.

Vocabulary and speaking

1 Replace the underlined words with the words in the box.

'in-crowd' lost touch keep in touch confide in a shoulder to cry on
turn to circle of friends

1 Have you <u>lost contact</u> with any of your old friends because you haven't written to them or called them?
2 Who do you <u>ask for help</u> when you need <u>sympathy</u>?
3 Who can you <u>tell secrets to and trust to keep them quiet</u>?
4 Are you the sort of person who likes to be in with the <u>fashionable people</u>?
5 In your <u>group of friends</u> does everybody have similar personalities?
6 How do you <u>stay in contact</u> with your friends?

2 Work with a partner. Ask and answer the questions in Ex 1.

LANGUAGE STUDY

Reporting on a survey

1 Look at these extracts from the text. Complete the table with the words and phrases in **bold**.

1 *You have 33 friends now,* **yet** *within a few years you will have lost touch with all but a handful.*

2 **According to the survey,** *best friends are not even the ones you see most of,* **but** *they are the ones you think of more often than any other.*

3 **The research identified** *four categories of friendship.*

4 *Pruners* **have a tendency towards** *making friends quickly.*

5 *Harvesters have a hardcore circle of friends* **despite** *spending long periods making no attempt to meet them.*

6 *Gatherers* **tend to** *make friends easily.*

7 *Men* **are more likely to** *be gatherers or harvesters,* **whereas** *women dominate the cultivator category.*

8 **One in three** *people admit they have 'silent' friends.*

9 **Despite** *the drop-out rate of friends,* **six out of ten** *people claimed they value their friendships more than money.*

Expressing contrast	Expressing tendency	Giving statistics	Referring to a study / survey
yet	*are less likely to*	*more than half*	*The study revealed*
1 _____	4 _____	7 _____	9 _____
2 _____	5 _____	8 _____	10 _____
3 _____	6 _____		

Grammar reference page 26

2 These findings are from a survey of British under-30s. Complete them with appropriate words and phrases from the table in Ex 1.

1 90% of teenagers say they would turn first to their parents for advice on most subjects _despite_ the age difference.

2 _According_ , 27% of twenty-somethings are parents.

3 Six out of ten under-30s are against marriage, _yet_ up-to-date statistics show that more people than ever are getting married.

4 Women _have a_ prefer their partners to be older than themselves, _____ men prefer their partners to be younger.

5 Men spend twice as much time surfing the internet as women, _____ women spend twice as much time as men watching TV soaps.

6 _It_ that one in three has admitted to breaking the law _____ agreeing that it was totally wrong to do so.

7 33% of women said they would consider cosmetic surgery, _whereas_ only 10% of men said they would ever consider it.

8 3% of over-18s _____ vote in a reality TV show than in a political election.
are more likely

3 Do you think the findings in Ex 2 would be similar in your country?

4 Turn to page 29 to conduct your own survey and to report your findings.

The word on the street

Listening and speaking   **1**   You are going to listen to five short interviews with women on what they look for in a partner. What do you think they will say?

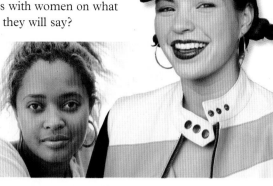

Victoria	Emma	Marie	Nadine	Laura
Looks ☐	Looks ☐	Looks ☐	Looks ☐	Looks ☐
Personality ☐	Personality ☐	Personality ☐	Personality ☐	Personality ☐

2   💿 **07** Listen to the interviews and tick one or both of the boxes. Did anything surprise you about the results of the survey?

3   Complete these extracts from the interviews with the words and expressions in the box. Then listen again and check your answers.

> up top   full of themselves   God's gift to women   really good-looking   toned
> the way he dresses

1   The one thing I can't stand is men who are really _____ – it puts me right off.
2   What I look for in a partner is warmth, intelligence, a good sense of humour … and a _____ body.
3   It's no good if they're _____ but really annoying.
4   What really annoys me is good-looking men who think they're _____.
5   The first thing I notice about a man is _____.
6   If he's really gorgeous, it doesn't matter what's _____, does it?

4   Match the words and expressions in Ex 3 to the definitions in the box.

> the style of his clothes   arrogant   in their head   slim, firm
> very attractive   everything a woman wants

5   Work with a partner. Do you agree or disagree with the statements in Ex 3? If you are male, discuss the statements as if they were about women.

6   Work in groups. Make a sentence about one of the topics in the box using the language in the table. The people in the group guess whether your sentence is true or false.

Example: *What I really hate about work is getting up in the mornings.*

> work   people   men   women   going out   learning English   fashion

What I One thing I	really	love / hate / can't stand / enjoy / don't understand	about … is …
What		irritates / annoys / interests / me fascinates / amazes	

 **CD-ROM**   For more activities go to **People Unit 2**

3 You're as old as you feel

The secret of a long life

Lead-in

1 Work with a partner. Look at the chart and guess how many years your lifestyle can add or take off your life. Complete the chart with the numbers.

+9   +7   +5   +4
+2   +6 months
-10   -10   -9
-4   -3   -2

What's good		And what's not	
good friends	+9	heavy drinking	-10
owning a pet	___	unhappy marriage	___
high social class	___	leaving school early	___
happy marriage	___	being overweight	___
positive personality	___	living near a main road	___
good diet	___	smoking	___

Listening and speaking

1 Answer these questions about the oldest person you know who is still in good health. Then tell your partner about him / her.

1 What did he / she do when he / she was younger?
2 What's his / her life like now and how does he / she stay healthy?

2 08 Listen to the radio interview about Maurice Anasse. Which of the things in the *What's good* list in Lead-in Ex 1 does the interview mention?

3 Are these statements true or false? If they are false, say why. Listen again and check your answers.

1 Maurice owned the first car in his village. ☐

2 Nowadays he gets his exercise by cycling. ☐

3 He uses the internet. ☐

4 He's never drunk alcohol or smoked. ☐

5 He used to make furniture for a living. ☐

6 He's an only child. ☐

7 Maurice thinks the secret of his longevity is to do with the inner self. ☐

4 Work with a partner and discuss these questions.

1 Maurice talks about taking every opportunity to do something new. When did you last do something for the first time?
2 Think of three things that you would like to do that you haven't done before.

Vocabulary

1 Work with a partner. Explain what the phrases in *italics* mean.

1 If you want to *live to a ripe old age* you need to …
2 When I'm old I'll *keep my mind active* by …
3 I don't think I'll reach *my late nineties* unless I …
4 The oldest member of my family who's *still going strong* is …
5 I …, but only *in moderation*.
6 … is *in the genes* in my family.

2 Complete the sentences in Ex 1 so that they are true for you. Then compare your ideas with a partner.

LANGUAGE STUDY

Uses of the infinitive

1   Look at these extracts from the radio interview. Match the examples in **bold** to the uses of the infinitive a–d.

1   *He says if you **want to live** to a ripe old age, you **need to keep** moving …*
2   *… and take every **opportunity to do** something new.*
3   *His **secret is to live** calmly and treat other people well.*
4   *Scientists have examined him and they're **desperate to find** a genetic explanation.*

a   verb + infinitive ☐   c   noun + infinitive ☐

b   adjective + infinitive ☐   d   noun + *be* + infinitive ☐

Grammar reference page 27

2   Complete this advice from centenarians on how to live to 100 using the words in the box.

> advice / stay   busy / help   chance / exercise   effort / walk   ~~essential / eat~~
> learn / play   secret / take   tend / live   time / see   try / get

Example: It's *essential to eat* sensibly and drink only in moderation.

1   I _____ exactly seven hours' sleep every night – no more and no less.
2   Make sure you're never too _____ anyone who needs it.
3   My _____ is _____ calm and relaxed at all times.
4   _____ a musical instrument. A musical life is a happier and longer life.
5   Make the _____ at least half a mile each day.
6   Never miss the _____ your brain – read, play games and take up new hobbies.
7   Find something to believe in. They say that spiritual people _____ longer.
8   Find the _____ your friends regularly. And keep up with the latest gossip.
9   The _____ is _____ things day by day and never worry about the future.

3   How many true sentences can you make using the words in the table?

Example: *I try to work hard and play hard.*

I (don't)	try tend		drink lots of water. work hard and play hard. exercise every day.
I'm (not)	reluctant willing	to	act older / younger than my / your age. have friends who are older than me / you. take my / your parents' advice.
It's (not)	a good idea a mistake easy important		get married before I'm / you're 30. give up everything that's bad for me / you. spend time with elderly relatives. take myself / yourself too seriously.

4   Work with a partner. Choose one of the topics in the box and give each other advice using the sentence beginnings 1–6. Do you agree with the advice?

> learning English   finding a boy / girlfriend   getting a job   being popular
> staying fit and healthy

1   It's important to …   4   Try to …
2   Take every opportunity to …   5   It's sensible to …
3   It's a good idea to …   6   The secret is to …

Reading **1** Look at the photos and answer the questions using the words in the box.

soul	pop	reggae	rock	metal	country	punk

1 What kind of music do you associate with each of the singers?
2 What age groups do they appeal to?
3 Who are your favourite singers and what style of music do they sing?

2 🎧 **09** Read the article about singer Joss Stone, which appeared when she released her first album at the age of 16. Match these headings to the paragraphs in the article.

1 How did she get started? ☐   5 Who does she mix with? ☐
2 How does she answer her critics? ☐   6 What do her critics say? ☐
3 Who is she? 1   7 What does the future hold? ☐
4 Has she made her fortune yet? ☐   8 What's she like? ☐

3 Work with a partner. Answer the questions in Ex 2 from memory and then check your answers in the text.

An old head on young shoulders

'Devon sent' by Polly Vernon for *The Observer Magazine OM* and 'Tangled up in blue' by Peter Lyle for *iD*

1 Joss Stone is a 16-year-old soul singer whose debut album has already charmed the music press. Tom Cruise loved her album so much that he constantly plays it in his car. (He's a bit on the mature side for her, but her mum's impressed!)

2 More Britney than Whitney – until she sings. When the innocent-looking teenager opens her mouth to sing, people expect her to sound like Britney Spears. But the sensuous, throaty roar of her singing voice sounds more like a black soul-diva or a jaded, forty-something divorcée.

3 At the age of 13, Joss hated school and needed to find a way out of it. 'I was really bad at it. My parents were like, "OK, but you're going to have to do something, Joss."'So she did. She entered a TV talent show and much to her surprise she won. She signed up with a record company shortly afterwards.

4 Surely she's much too young and innocent to sing lyrics that are full of references to the ups and downs of life experience? How can she know the heartache and pain of which she sings?

5 'I'm 16 years old! My heart's been broken loads of times. I don't understand why it matters how old I am,' she says. 'I mean, like, how old do you have to be to feel any emotion at all? I mean, just because I'm not very old doesn't mean I've been wrapped up in cotton wool. People forget what it was like to be young. For me it's like, "I want to change the world."'

6 Does she feel rich? 'No, because I'm not. My mum's looking after the money. I don't get it until I'm in my twenties. You should ask my mum if she feels rich.'

7 She's working on an album of original material, due for release later this year. 'Am I ambitious? Yeah, I think so. I want to make something of myself.' She does not have any other specific ambitions – she says, 'just sing anywhere and meet new people and be successful, I suppose.'

8 In many ways Joss is just like any other teenager, but, unlike most teenagers, she now rubs shoulders with people in high places. She's met George Bush twice. 'We were chatting away,' she says, 'And I'm like, "Hey, how's it going being president?" And he said, "It's great." He reminded me of somebody I lived next door to back home. He's like a farmer.'

Vocabulary

1 Replace the <u>underlined</u> words with words and phrases used in the text.

1 Joss Stone <u>captivated</u> the music press with her first album. (paragraph 1)

2 Tom Cruise played it in his car <u>all the time</u>. (paragraph 1)

3 Her singing voice sounds like a <u>tired, cynical</u> woman in her forties. (paragraph 2)

4 After winning a TV talent show, she <u>got a contract</u> with a record company. (paragraph 3)

5 In answer to people who think she's too young to have any life experience, she says that she may be young but she hasn't <u>led a sheltered life</u>. (paragraph 5)

6 Her album of original material <u>is going to go on sale</u> later this year. (paragraph 7)

2 Match the <u>underlined</u> examples of *like* to the definitions in the box.

a *say / said*	**b** to draw attention to what you are going to say	**c** *similar to*

1 People expect her to sound <u>like</u> Britney Spears. ☐ *c*

2 'My parents <u>were like</u>, "OK, but you're going to have to do something, Joss."' ☐

3 'I mean, <u>like</u>, how old do you have to be to feel any emotion at all?' ☐

4 'For me it's <u>like</u>, "I want to change the world."' ☐

5 'We were chatting away,' she says, 'And <u>I'm like</u>, "Hey, how's it going being president?"' ☐

6 'He's <u>like</u> a farmer.' ☐

3 Which two uses of *like* in Ex 2 are very informal? Which use is neutral?

Speaking

1 What age do you associate with each of the activities in box A? Discuss your ideas with a partner using the age expressions in box B.

> **A**
> getting a tattoo   getting married   having a broken heart   doing yoga
> going to discos   leaving home   knitting   learning to drive   snowboarding
> texting   reading the newspaper   buying a house   gardening   having children

> **B**
> teens, twenties, thirties, forties, etc   twenty-something, thirty-something, etc
> early twenties, mid-thirties, late forties, etc   middle-aged   old age

2 🔘 **10** Listen to five people talking about the best age to get married and try to visualise the speakers. Note down what you think their age is and what they look like. Then compare your ideas with a partner.

3 Turn to page 32 to see photos of the people. How similar or different are they from your ideas in Ex 2?

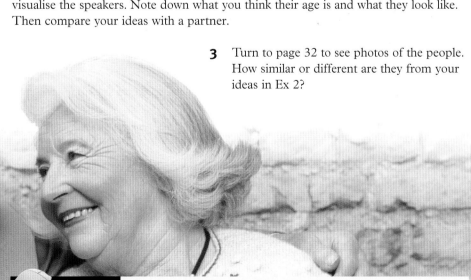

4 A dream job

LEARNING AIMS

- Can talk about real and hypothetical situations
- Can use job vocabulary and discuss dream jobs
- Can write a CV

Follow your dreams

Lead-in **1** Spend two minutes thinking about this question and then discuss it in small groups.

If you had unlimited talents and abilities, what would you do?

Reading and vocabulary **1** Work with a partner. Decide if the feeelings in the box are positive or negative.

captivated   crushed   humiliated   depressed   enthusiastic   excited
exhilarated   scared

2 🔊 **11** Read the story about Jean Harper on page 15. What made her experience the feelings in Ex 1?

Example: *She was captivated by airplanes and flying.*

3 Are these statements about Jean true or false?

1 At school she had no idea what she wanted to do when she <u>became an adult</u>. (line 3)

2 She was <u>raised and educated</u> in a farming community. (line 5)

3 She was <u>discouraged</u> by the negative attitude of some of her teachers and classmates. (line 19)

4 Although it was difficult to keep believing in her dream, she never <u>stopped trying</u>. (line 28)

5 Her teacher in her senior year encouraged her to <u>try to fulfil</u> her dreams. (line 58)

6 One day she <u>approached</u> her senior teacher's desk and slapped her. (line 63)

7 She <u>succeeded in achieving</u> everything her third grade teacher had said she couldn't do. (line 68)

4 Replace the <u>underlined</u> words in Ex 3 with phrasal verbs from the text about Jean.

5 Put the lines of this summary of Jean's life in the correct order.

a for the impossible?' she thought. But despite being brought ☐

b down and she lost all enthusiasm. She eventually gave ☐

c Young Jean knew what she wanted to do when she was growing ☐1☐

d up all hope that she could do anything interesting. 'Why go ☐

e on to become the pilot she had always wanted to be. ☐

f up by supportive parents, it was thanks to another teacher that she went ☐

g up, but her third grade teacher's negative attitude beat her ☐

6 Work with a partner. Look at this extract from the text and discuss the questions.

'If you abandon your dreams, you'll regret it forever. You can have whatever you want if you want it enough.'

1 Who do you know who has followed their dreams and succeeded?

2 Do you believe it's possible to have whatever you want if you want it enough?

The wind beneath her wings

'Wind Beneath Her Wings' by Carol Kline in *Chicken Soup for a Woman's Soul*, published by *Health Communications Inc*

When Jean Harper was in her third grade, her teacher gave the class an assignment on what they wanted to be when they grew up. Jean's father was a pilot in the little farming
5   community where she was brought up and Jean was totally captivated by airplanes and flying. She poured her heart into her report and included all of her dreams: she wanted to make parachute jumps and be an airline pilot. Her
10 paper came back with an 'F' on it. The teacher told her it was a 'fairy tale' and that none of the occupations she listed were women's jobs. Jean was crushed and humiliated.

She showed her father the paper and he told her that of course she could become a pilot. But as the years went by, Jean was beaten down by the negativity she encountered whenever she talked about her career – 'Girls can't become airline pilots;
25 never have, never will.' – until, feeling totally depressed, she finally gave up.

In her senior year of high school, her English teacher was a Mrs Dorothy Slaton, an uncompromising, demanding teacher with high standards and a low tolerance for excuses. One day,

Mrs Slaton gave the class an assignment. 'What
40 do you think you'll be doing ten years from now?' Jean thought about the assignment. Pilot? No way. Flight attendant? I'm not pretty enough – they'd never accept me. Wife? What guy would want me? Waitress? I could do *that*. That
45 felt safe, so she wrote it down.

Two weeks later, the teacher handed back the assignments, face down on each desk, and asked this question: 'If you had unlimited talents and abilities, what would you do?' Jean felt a
50 rush of the old enthusiasm, and with excitement she wrote down all her old dreams. When the students stopped writing, the teacher asked, 'How many students wrote the same thing on both sides of the paper?' Not one hand went up.

55 The next thing that Mrs Slaton said changed the course of Jean's life. 'I have a little secret for you all. You do have unlimited abilities and talents. If you don't go for your dreams, no one will do it for you. And if you abandon your
60 dreams, you'll regret it forever. You can have whatever you want if you want it enough.'

Jean felt exhilarated and a little scared. She went up to the teacher's desk and told Mrs Slaton about her dream of becoming a pilot.
65 Mrs Slaton slapped the desk. 'If you want to be a pilot, then do it!' she said.

So Jean did. It took ten years of hard work and facing opposition. But she went on to do everything her third-grade teacher said was a
70 fairy tale. Today, Jean Harper is a Boeing 757 captain for United Airlines.

LANGUAGE STUDY

Real and hypothetical situations

1   Look at these sentences from the text about Jean.
   1   *If you **had** unlimited talents and abilities, what **would** you do?*
   2   *If you **abandon** your dreams, you'**ll** regret it forever.*
   3   *You **can** have whatever you want if you **want** it enough.*
   4   *If you **want** to be a pilot, then **do** it!*

   In which of the sentences is the speaker talking about a situation she sees as:

   a   real and possible? ☐ ☐ ☐   b   unreal and hypothetical? ☐

2   In the sentences that express a real situation:
   a   which tense is used in the *if* clause?   b   which structures are used in the main clause?

3   In the sentence that expresses an unreal situation:
   a   which tense is used in the *if* clause?   b   which modal verb is used in the main clause?

Grammar reference page 27

4   Correct one mistake in each of these sentences.

   Example: If I ~~would have~~ the chance, I'd love to live and work abroad one day.
   (had)

   1   Things would be a lot better if I don't have so much work to do.

   2   I'll be so pleased if we won't get any homework tonight.

   3   If I would have more time, I'd read a lot more.

   4   If I can find the time, I go shopping tomorrow.

   5   I wouldn't be surprised if I would fail my exam next month.

   6   If only I could, I give up work tomorrow.

   7   If I will need advice about anything, the first person I talk to is my best friend.

5   Change the endings of the sentences in Ex 4 to make them true for you. Then compare your ideas with a partner.

   Example: If I had the chance, I'd *stop working for a year and go travelling.*

6   Match the beginnings and endings of these quotations. Then choose your favourite three and compare your ideas with a partner.

   1   If you tell the truth,
   2   It is amazing what you can accomplish
   3   If you obey all the rules,
   4   Most people would succeed in small things
   5   Never continue in a job you don't enjoy. If you're happy in what you're doing,

   a   if you don't care who gets the credit. *Harry S Truman, US president*
   b   you don't have to remember anything. *Mark Twain, writer*
   c   if they were not troubled with great ambitions. *Henry Longfellow, poet*
   d   you'll like yourself, you'll have inner peace. *Johnny Carson, chat show host*
   e   you miss all the fun. *Katherine Hepburn, actress*

7   Complete these sentences to make them true for you. Then read your sentences to a partner and give each other some advice using *if* + imperative.

   Example: I want to … *improve my English.*
   If you want to improve your English, practise as much as possible.

   1   I want to …   4   I'm fed up with …
   2   I'm feeling …   5   I've got no …
   3   I can't stand …   6   I don't understand …

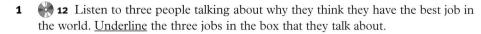

I'd love to do that

Listening and vocabulary

1  **12** Listen to three people talking about why they think they have the best job in the world. <u>Underline</u> the three jobs in the box that they talk about.

> computer game designer   hurricane hunter   extreme explorer   chocolate taster
> forensic chemist   kissing trainer for actors   skateboard test rider   movie star
> dream analyst   nightclub researcher   bed tester

2 One of the three jobs in Ex 1 is not real. Which do you think it is? Why?

3 Who said these things? Write G (George), R (Ronnie) or L (Lou) next to each extract. Then listen again and check your answers.

1   At the time I was <u>out of work</u>.
2   The job has its <u>perks</u>.
3   I don't work <u>nine to five</u>.
4   He kept turning up late so he was <u>sacked</u>.
5   You need a <u>degree</u> in science or maths.
6   Oh, and it's <u>well paid</u>, too.
7   I don't mind doing <u>overtime</u>.

4 Match the <u>underlined</u> words and phrases in Ex 3 to the definitions in the box.

> with a good salary   benefits   dismissed   university qualification
> unemployed   to a standard working timetable   extra work after normal hours

Speaking

1 Think about your dream job and answer these questions.

- What is the job?
- What skills and personal qualities do you need?
- Do you need any special qualifications?
- What does the job involve?
- What's the best thing about it?
- Are there any downsides?
- Why is this your dream job?

2 Work in groups. Interview the other people in your group about their dream job.

Writing

1 Read the tips on how to write a good curriculum vitae.

The perfect graduate CV

General	Give facts and avoid negative information. Put a positive spin on facts, but always tell the truth. Enclose an appropriate photo or no photo at all.
Style	Clear layout is essential. Use good-quality, plain white paper, wide margins, and bold type for headings.
Contact details	Prospective employers are busy people – make it easy for them to contact you. Do not include sex or marital status. Do include mobile number and email address.
Skills	Use positive language, eg *experienced in …, extensive knowledge of …, fluent / adequate speaker of …*
Education and qualifications	List in chronological order, starting with the most recent. Don't include primary school.
Previous employment	Give details of your responsibilities and achievements, eg *I have experience in …, I am trained in …, I managed …, I developed …, I implemented …, I created …*
Hobbies and interests	If you are a recent graduate, and have little in the way of work experience, it's important to show how your leisure interests reflect your good qualities. For example, team sports show that you are a team-player while other activities show that you are versatile or have leadership qualities. Use terminology that indicates that you are alive and have energy. Above all show passion. Make it clear that when you commit to something, you really go for it.

2 Turn to page 32 and find at least six ways to improve the example CV.

3 Write your CV following the advice in the tips.

CD-ROM   For more activities go to **People Unit 4**

5 Review

Lead-in   1   Are talent shows / contests popular in your country? What sort of people enter them?

People and jobs

1   ⊙ **13**   Sam, Lisa and Camellia are finalists in the talent contest *Teen idol*. Listen to the judges' opinions and complete this sentence.

The judges think that (1) _____ is a go-getter, (2) _____ is a bit of a clown and (3) _____ is a team-player.

2   Who do these adjectives refer to? Write S (Sam), L (Lisa) or C (Camellia). Listen again and check.

1 ambitious ☐   2 creative ☐   3 dependable ☐   4 energetic ☐   5 dull ☐

6 entertaining ☐   7 level-headed ☐   8 enthusiastic ☐   9 self-confident ☐

10 superficial ☐

3   ⊙ **14**   Who do you think won? Listen to the judges' final opinion and check.

4   Think of some famous singers, actors or other entertainers who can be described with the words in Ex 2. What other adjectives can you use to describe these people? Discuss your ideas with a partner.

5   Replace the <u>underlined</u> words and phrases with the words and phrases in the box.

| degree   overtime   perks   nine to five   out of work   sacked   well paid |

1   The most important factor for me in a job? That it's <u>got a good salary</u>.
2   Of course, I would hope my job had some <u>benefits</u> like a company car.
3   If I was always late for work, I would expect to be <u>asked to leave</u>.
4   Having practical experience is more important than having a <u>university qualification</u>.
5   I would prefer to choose my own hours than to have to work <u>to a standard timetable</u>.
6   I'd like a job with lots of opportunities to do <u>extra work</u>.
7   I would rather be <u>unemployed</u> than have a job I hate.

6   Tick the statements in Ex 5 that you agree with. Discuss your ideas with a partner.

Famous at fifteen

1   Read the interview with Priscilla Prete, a young model from Argentina, and answer these questions.
1   Who does Priscilla <u>keep in touch with</u>?
2   Despite still being <u>a teenager</u>, what do her parents think about her living in the city?
3   What's <u>a natural characteristic</u> in Priscilla's family?
4   How does Priscilla describe her <u>group of friends</u>?
5   Who does Priscilla call when she needs <u>someone to listen to her problems</u>?
6   What does she do only <u>in a controlled way</u>?
7   Who does Priscilla want to see <u>living a long time</u>?

2   Replace the <u>underlined</u> expressions in Ex 1 with expressions Priscilla uses to talk about age and friendship.

3   Read the interview with Priscilla again and find examples of these uses of the infinitive.
1   verb + infinitive (4 examples)   3   noun + infinitive (4 examples)
2   adjective + infinitive (2 examples)

Priscilla Prete

'What's it like to be 15 in 2003' by Hero Brown, published by *Marie Claire*

Have you always wanted to be a model?
Yes, from when I was very little. I'd dress up and parade in front of people. I had no desire to do anything else.

Has modelling affected your life at all?
The biggest thing was moving to Buenos Aires from the village where I grew up. It's about 1,000 miles away. I attend a school in Buenos Aires, but I keep in close contact with my parents. They seem to understand that there are bad influences in the city, but they trust me even though I'm still in my teens.

Do you feel any pressure to be model thin?
For me, it's not a problem. It's easy to stay this shape. My family are all tall and slim – it's in our genes.

How has your success affected your friendships?
I have a large circle of friends and they have all been really supportive. I chose to leave my village but I still talk to my best friend from home every day on the phone.

What do you love and hate about Argentina?
I love how people came together during the economic crisis, but I hate seeing the effect of such difficult times. With so much unemployment, some people get beaten down and they just give up.

What can't you live without?
A telephone call to my parents (they're always eager to hear my news and I sometimes need a shoulder to cry on), food and a sense of humour.

How much do you spend on going out every month?
The only money I spend is on clothes. I never get an overwhelming urge to spend lots of money – everything in moderation.

How important is success to you?
I would like to be a successful model and that's what I'm going for right now. But I know true happiness will be in bringing up my children with my husband, looking after my house and living to a ripe old age.

4 Complete these sentences with an appropriate word from Ex 3. Which statements are true for you? Tell your partner.

1 I've always _____ to be a performer – you know, an actor or a musician.

2 I don't feel under _____ to be the best at everything I do.

3 I'm so _____ to earn a lot of money that I'd do pretty much any job.

4 I have no _____ to leave my home town and move away.

5 Complete these sentences with the correct form of the phrasal verbs in the box. Use each verb only once.

give up   bring up   go for   beat down   grow up

1 Priscilla _____ in a small village in Argentina.

2 She is looking forward one day to _____ her own children.

3 It made her sad to see some people get _____ and eventually _____ during the economic crisis.

4 She made her mind up that she was going to be a model and she _____ it.

6 Complete these sentences with the past simple, past continuous, past perfect simple / continuous.

1 Priscilla (spend) _____ the first 15 years of her life in a small village in Argentina.

2 She (study) _____ at high school when she started modelling in Buenos Aires.

3 When she was in her mid-teens, she (move) _____ to the capital city.

4 Before she was offered a place at a modelling agency, she (try) _____ for a long time to get accepted.

5 Priscilla (intend) _____ always _____ to become a model so she was happy when she was finally accepted.

7 Rewrite these sentences using the verbs in brackets.

1 I had intended to go travelling but my parents wouldn't let me. (was going to)

2 They expected me to pass all my exams, but I failed them instead. (was supposed to)

3 I should have been the captain of the rugby team, but I broke my leg. (was meant to)

What if ...?

1   Complete these sentences with advice on how to lead a healthier lifestyle.

1   If you're doing less than three hours exercise per week – *join a gym immediately.*
2   If you spend more than five hours a day at your computer, …
3   If you want to feel more positive about life, …
4   If you can't get to sleep at night, …
5   If you want to make yourself look more attractive, …

2   Work with a partner. Read your suggestions to each other. Choose the best piece of advice for each situation.

'Scruples'

1   Work in groups of three or four. Read how to play 'Scruples' and play the game.

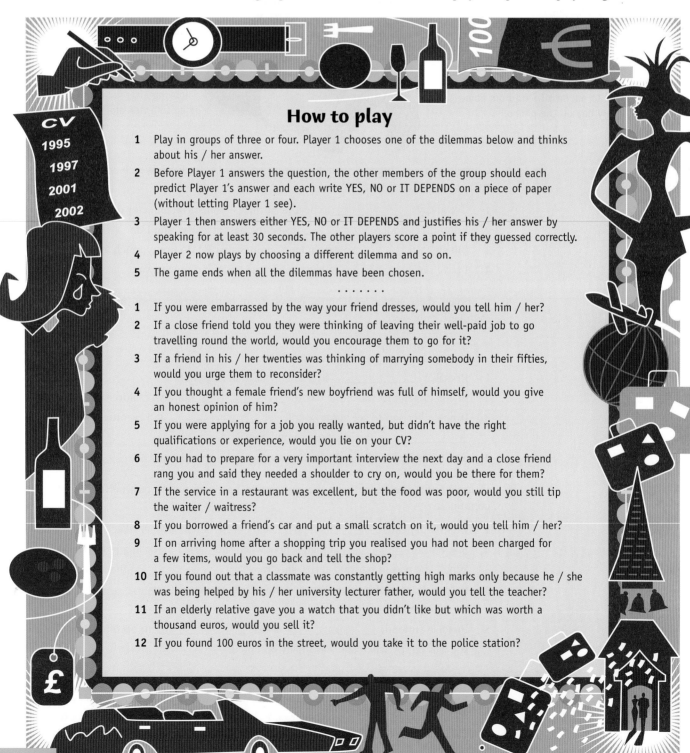

How to play

1   Play in groups of three or four. Player 1 chooses one of the dilemmas below and thinks about his / her answer.
2   Before Player 1 answers the question, the other members of the group should each predict Player 1's answer and each write YES, NO or IT DEPENDS on a piece of paper (without letting Player 1 see).
3   Player 1 then answers either YES, NO or IT DEPENDS and justifies his / her answer by speaking for at least 30 seconds. The other players score a point if they guessed correctly.
4   Player 2 now plays by choosing a different dilemma and so on.
5   The game ends when all the dilemmas have been chosen.

. . . .

1   If you were embarrassed by the way your friend dresses, would you tell him / her?
2   If a close friend told you they were thinking of leaving their well-paid job to go travelling round the world, would you encourage them to go for it?
3   If a friend in his / her twenties was thinking of marrying somebody in their fifties, would you urge them to reconsider?
4   If you thought a female friend's new boyfriend was full of himself, would you give an honest opinion of him?
5   If you were applying for a job you really wanted, but didn't have the right qualifications or experience, would you lie on your CV?
6   If you had to prepare for a very important interview the next day and a close friend rang you and said they needed a shoulder to cry on, would you be there for them?
7   If the service in a restaurant was excellent, but the food was poor, would you still tip the waiter / waitress?
8   If you borrowed a friend's car and put a small scratch on it, would you tell him / her?
9   If on arriving home after a shopping trip you realised you had not been charged for a few items, would you go back and tell the shop?
10   If you found out that a classmate was constantly getting high marks only because he / she was being helped by his / her university lecturer father, would you tell the teacher?
11   If an elderly relative gave you a watch that you didn't like but which was worth a thousand euros, would you sell it?
12   If you found 100 euros in the street, would you take it to the police station?

Otis Redding was born in 1941 in Macon, Georgia, USA. He was a soul singer with a strong voice, known for his passionate but tender delivery. His first recording *These arms of mine* was a hit in the early 1960s. It was followed a few years later by *Mr Pitiful, I can't turn you loose, (I can't get no) Satisfaction* (the Rolling Stones song) and *Respect* (later a hit for Aretha Franklin). Although it was unusual for singers to write their songs at the time, Redding wrote many of his own. In 1967 he played at the hugely influential Monterey Pop Festival in California and received rave reviews. However, six months later Otis Redding and his backing band died in a plane crash. His most famous song, *(Sittin' on) The dock of the bay*, became famous a year later. Despite only reaching the age of 26, Otis Redding had, and continues to have, a profound effect on the world of soul music.

Song

1   Read the factfile about Otis Redding and answer these questions.

    1   What was his debut recording called?
    2   Who wrote most of his songs?
    3   Which song is he best known for?

2   🔘 **15** Match the two halves of each line of the song. Then listen and check.

That's how strong my love is

1   1   If I was the sun,   **a**   love most everywhere
    2   I'd go with   **b**   that I'm still around
    3   I'll be the moon   **c**   way up there
    4   Just to let you know   **d**   when the sun goes down

Chorus
That's how strong my love is

2   1   I'll be the weeping willow   **a**   swimming when you're here
    2   And you can go   **b**   drowning in my tears
    3   I'll be the rainbow   **c**   and keep you warm
    4   Wrap you in my colours   **d**   after the tears are gone

Chorus

3   1   I'll be the ocean,   **a**   and love you warm
    2   And catch all the tears   **b**   after the storm is gone
    3   I'll be the breeze   **c**   whenever you cry
    4   To dry your eyes   **d**   so deep and wide

Chorus

3   Who would you sing this song to, a boy / girlfriend, a member of your family or anyone else? Compare your ideas with a partner.

4   Write one more verse dedicated to whoever you chose in Ex 3.
    If I was …   I'd …   I'll be …   Just to …

Extra practice

Unit 1

1 Find eleven character adjectives and match them to the definitions below. The words go →, ↓ and ↘.

B	G	A	S	S	E	R	T	I	V	E	L	U
E	S	I	M	P	U	L	S	I	V	E	Y	N
N	H	U	V	B	X	R	J	K	L	B	R	F
T	F	C	P	F	I	B	V	D	S	Y	A	L
H	R	H	X	E	Z	T	R	X	N	P	T	A
U	X	E	H	G	R	Q	I	G	S	K	I	P
S	Z	E	Y	J	Q	F	F	O	H	Z	O	P
I	G	R	E	G	A	R	I	O	U	S	N	A
A	S	F	P	F	R	B	V	C	Z	S	A	B
S	Q	U	T	N	C	H	M	L	I	H	L	L
T	O	L	E	R	A	N	T	T	Z	A	N	E
I	K	B	D	E	P	E	N	D	A	B	L	E
C	O	N	V	E	N	T	I	O	N	A	L	X

Hint: All the vowels are part of a word.

Example: wants to be successful _ambitious_

1 acts without thinking _____
2 makes sensible decisions _____
3 follows the norm _____
4 always stays calm _____
5 will always be there for you _____
6 is happy and positive _____
7 likes to show authority _____
8 accepting of others' beliefs _____
9 very interested / excited about things _____
10 likes to be with other people _____
11 does not think about serious / important things

_____

2 Mark the main stress on the words in Ex 1.
Example: _ambitious_

3 Complete these sentences with the expressions in the box.

> go-getter   team-player   bit of a clown
> bit of a loner

1 He's generally quite serious, but he can be a _____ at times.
2 He'll go a long way. He's very ambitious and determined – definitely a _____.
3 She's a _____ actually. She seems to prefer being by herself a lot of the time.
4 She works well on her own, but at the same time she's also definitely a _____.

4 Complete this text with the correct past form of the verbs.

'I (1 apply) _____ for loads of jobs already, with no luck whatsoever, when I finally (2 come across) _____ an ad for the perfect job. I (3 know) _____ there would be a lot of competition, so while I (4 drive) _____ to the interview, I (5 come up with) _____ what (6 suppose) _____ to be the perfect plan. So, we (7 chat) _____ away during the interview when right on cue my mobile (8 ring) _____.
I (9 apologise) _____, asking if it was OK to take the call, and I then (10 start) _____ saying into the phone things like, "Which company? When do I start? How much? Wow! And a car!". When I (11 finish) _____ the call, rather than being impressed, the interviewers just (12 laugh) _____ and said they (13 interview) _____ another guy trying to pull the same stunt the day before. I (14 not / get) _____ the job.'

5 Complete these sentences with the verbs in brackets and appropriate endings.

Example: I (go / ask) _was going to ask_ this girl out on a date, but she _already had a boyfriend_.

1 We (go / revise) _____ for our exams last weekend, but _____.
2 The interviewer (meant / be) _____ very tough, but _____.
3 I (supposed / give) _____ an important presentation yesterday, but _____ _____.
4 Our first date (meant / be) _____ very romantic, but _____.
5 The course I signed up for (supposed / be) _____ very practical, but _____ _____.

6 Think of something that has recently not gone according to plan for you. Write a brief email to a friend telling them about it.

Unit 2

1 Complete these sentences with the prepositions in the box.

> of / in   to / on   to / with   out / in   in / up

1 Even though we've fallen _____ a few times, my best friend is still the only person I can confide _____ about anything.

2 I don't know what it is about me, but my friends always seem to turn _____ me when they need a shoulder to cry _____.

3 I suppose I've got quite a wide circle _____ friends, but I've never been interested in being part of the ' _____-crowd'.

4 It's sometimes hard to keep _____ touch with old friends, but I usually manage to catch _____ with them via email.

5 I got _____ know lots of people at school, but I've lost contact _____ most of them now.

2 Match the beginnings to the ends of these expressions. Does each expression have a positive or negative meaning?

1	He hasn't got much up	a	looking.
2	He's really good-	b	women.
3	He is so full of	c	top.
4	He thinks he's God's gift to	d	himself.

3 Write the name of a famous person who fits each of the descriptions in Ex 2.

1 _____   3 _____

2 _____   4 _____

4 Complete this article with the words and phrases in the box.

> according to a recent survey   nine out of ten
> according to the survey   but   likely to   tend to
> more than half of   the study revealed   whereas

The cyber generation – connected, career-minded and confident

(1) _____, the cyber generation, people born since 1980, are connected, career-minded and confident.

(2) _____ that almost 100 percent of the cyber generation is online. In contrast with their parents' generation, the internet is their main source of information and news with (3) _____ turning first to their computers for the information they need. They communicate with each other through cyberspace and most are (4) _____ send several emails and texts every day. They (5) _____ organise their social lives without even speaking to each other and for some, the internet and texting is their social life.

(6) _____ , the 'dream job' for (7) _____ the cyber generation is to have their own e-company. They want lots of responsibility, independence and flexible working hours, (8) _____ they say that prestige and a high salary is not so important for them.

(9) _____ older generations struggle to come to terms with the internet, the cyber generation believes that the net has brought them closer to each other and to the world.

5 The following competition appeared in an IT magazine. Write your entry in no more than 150 words.

Tell us how you use the internet and

WIN A COMPUTER

Unit 3

1 Complete the article with the words and phrases in the box.

> life expectancy   in the genes   longevity
> ripe old age   still be going strong

Today's child may live to be 130

Children born at the beginning of the 21st century could (1) _____ at 130. The age to which humans can live is increasing all the time and scientists now believe there is no biological limit to ageing. Improved public health and developments in medical technology are the main reasons for increased (2) _____.

A recent study showed that (3) _____ is now increasing at over one year per decade and if this continues, the average maximum age will be 120 by the year 2120. It is very likely that some people will live at least ten years longer than this and reach the (4) _____ of 130. Advances in science and medicine may increase this average age even more.

So, is long life also (5) _____? It certainly is as far as your sex is concerned; 90% of all centenarians are women.

average maximum age = the average age at which the oldest few per cent of people die

2 Complete these phrases with *He's*, *He's a* or *He's in his*.

1 _____ teenager.
2 _____ twenty-something.
3 _____ middle-aged.
4 _____ late teens.
5 _____ mid-thirties.
6 _____ thirtyish.
7 _____ early sixties.
8 _____ elderly.
9 _____ fifties.

3 Put the ages in Ex 2 into order from youngest to oldest.

4 Write the name of a person you know who is each of the ages in Ex 2.

1 _____
2 _____
3 _____
4 _____
5 _____
6 _____
7 _____
8 _____
9 _____

5 Complete these dialogues with the pairs of words and the infinitive.

> easy / use   ~~ready / go~~   ask / wait
> arrange / meet up   surprised / see   manage / find
> time / walk   want / come out   way / get

1 **A:** Are you (1) _ready to go_ _____? The taxi is here.

 B: Hang on. Can you (2) _____ him _____ for a few minutes?

2 **A:** I was (3) _____ Sara at the party last night. I haven't seen her for ages.

 B: Yes, she's been away. Actually, we're going to (4) _____ some time next week. Do you (5) _____ with us?

3 **A:** I like your new camera. Is it (6) _____?

 B: When I (7) _____ the instruction manual, I'll let you know!

4 **A:** Can you tell me the best (8) _____ to the city centre?

 B: If you've got (9) _____ , it's a lovely stroll along the river.

6 Your friend is planning his / her 21st birthday party. Complete these sentences with some good advice.

1 It would be a good idea to _____ _____.

2 You should try to _____ _____.

3 It's not necessary to _____ _____.

4 It's absolutely essential to _____ _____.

5 It's better not to _____ _____.

6 The most important thing is to _____ _____.

Unit 4

1 Cross out the alternative that has a different meaning.

1 I've never been *unemployed* / *out of work* / *in employment*.

2 My new job has got lots of *disadvantages* / *benefits* / *perks*.

3 I'd hate to work *nine to five* / *flexi-time* / *regular hours*.

4 I've never been *sacked* / *promoted* / *fired*.

5 I need a job *that is well paid* / *with a good salary* / *that pays peanuts*.

6 I'm usually happy to work *extra time* / *overtime* / *extra hours*.

2 Match these words to the definitions.

1	captivated	a	afraid or frightened
2	crushed	b	embarrassed and ashamed
3	discouraged	c	very attracted and interested
4	exhilarated	d	feeling less confident
5	humiliated	e	totally defeated
6	scared	f	happy, excited and full of energy

3 Use the words in Ex 2 to describe how somebody might feel in these situations.

1 They fail an important exam.

_____

2 They are watching a fantastic film.

_____

3 They are skiing.

_____

4 Their boy / girlfriend leaves them.

_____

5 They are watching some bad news on TV.

_____

6 They are criticised in public.

_____

4 Complete this profile with the correct form of the phrasal verbs in the box. Who is the person?

give up	bring up	go for	go on to
set up	grow up		

5 Complete these internet ads with the most appropriate form of the verbs.

1
If ever you (feel) _____ stressed-out at work, (visit) _____ www.stressbusterlondon.co.uk for a tension-releasing massage at your desk within 30 minutes.

2
If you (look) _____ for a new line of work, you (find) _____ a wide variety of jobs at www.justthejob.com.

3
If you (can) _____ have any job in the world, what (be) _____ it _____ ? Email me today and that job will be yours tomorrow. www.bill@dreamjobs.com

4
www.thisjobs4u.com is in daily contact with over 10,000 businesses looking for the right person. If you (visit) _____ us today, you (never / look) _____ back.

5
If you (have got) _____ a computer at home, then (log on) _____ to www.earnthousands.com and you'll soon be earning in excess of £1,000 a week.

6
If you (be) _____ 100% happy in your job, you (not / read) _____ this ad right now. But you are, so do something about it! www.rightjobforyou.com

He was born in 1950 and (1) _____ in Surrey, UK. He was (2) _____ by his lawyer father and his mother, who was an airline stewardess. At the age of 16, while still at school, he started a national student magazine and a student advisory service. At 18, he decided to (3) _____ studying to (4) _____ his dream of working in the music industry, first selling records by mail order and then opening a record shop in London. He formed his record company in 1972 and sold it to EMI in 1992. In 1984, he (5) _____ an airline company, which (6) _____ become one of the biggest in the world. Among his many other business ventures are a mobile phone and an internet company. He was knighted 'Sir Richard' in 1999.

He is _____.

Grammar reference

Unit 1

Talking about the past

Past simple

You use the past simple to talk about a completed event in the past. The time reference is either given or is clear from the context:

*I **got** my first job in 2004.*

***Did** you **get** the job?* (that you applied for last week)

In narratives, you often use the past simple to talk about the key events of the story:

*I **had** my ear right up against the door for the third interview and I **jotted down** the questions and answers.*

Past continuous

You use the past continuous to talk about an activity in progress at a certain time in the past. You often use it to give the background in a narrative:

*I **was waiting** with the others outside the interview room.*

You also use the past continuous to describe an action in progress when another action happened:

*About halfway through, as we **were chatting away**, he came in.*

Past perfect simple and continuous

You use the past perfect to talk about an event or activity that took place before another event in the past or before the time of the main events of the story:

*The interview was supposed to be with a man and a woman, but he**'d been held up** in traffic.*

You use the past perfect continuous to show that an activity was in progress over a period of time:

*By the time they called me, I**'d been waiting** for ages.*

be supposed to / be meant to / be going to

Form

was / were	supposed to meant to going to	infinitive

Use

You can use *was / were supposed to*, *was / were meant to* and *was / were going to* to talk about an event or situation that was intended or predicted, but which didn't happen as planned or predicted:

*The interview **was supposed to** be with a man and a woman, but he'd been held up in traffic.*
*We **were meant to** take off at 10.30, but the flight was late.*
*I **was going to** phone you earlier, but I just didn't have time.*

Unit 2

Reporting on a survey

Expressing contrast

But is the most common contrastive linker in English:
*Most of us own a mobile, **but** only a few of us use it every day.*

Yet emphasises that something is surprising:
*55% of Americans think guns should be outlawed, **yet** private gun ownership is at an all-time high.*

Whereas balances two contrasting facts or ideas. It can occur in the middle or at the beginning of a sentence:
***Whereas** men shop out of necessity, women shop for pleasure.*
*I like going to pubs **whereas** my girlfriend prefers wine bars.*

Despite and *in spite of* are followed by:
a the *-ing* form of a verb   **b** a noun
c the phrase *the fact that* + subject clause

They express that something happens even though something else makes it seem unlikely. They can occur in the middle or at the beginning of a sentence:

*Only 1% of adults regularly do any sport **despite** expressing major concerns about their fitness.*
***In spite of** the anti-smoking lobby, many people still smoke.*
*He won the match **despite the fact that** he'd been ill.*

Expressing tendency

Tend to and *be more / less likely to* are common expressions to express tendency:
*Women **tend to be** more romantic than men.*
*Men **are** much **more likely** than women **to enjoy** sport.*

Have a tendency towards + -ing is less common and usually expresses an aspect of behaviour or character:
*Older people **have a tendency towards being** cautious.*

Giving statistics

Here are some common examples of statistical language:

1 in 5   1 out of 5   20%
*7 **out of** 10 said they were happy with their job.*

most (of)   the majority / minority (of)   almost all (of)
less / more than half (of)   only a few (of)
***Only a** very **few** said they regretted relocating.*

You can use the following phrases for approximating:
just under / over   nearly   almost   approximately
roughly   getting on for
***Just over** 40% have an overseas holiday each year.*

Referring to a survey

Here are some examples of how to refer to a survey:
According to the study / research / survey, …
The study / research / survey shows / revealed / identifies …
***According to the study**, 1 in 20 of us is left-handed.*
***The survey revealed** that salaries have risen by 3.75%.*

Unit 3

Uses of the infinitive

Verbs

You use the infinitive after certain verbs:
*We **expect to arrive** at about nine.*
*He **promised** not **to tell** anyone.*

Sometimes the verbs take an object:
*My parents always **encouraged me to be independent**.*

Here are some verbs that can be followed by the infinitive.

> **Without an object**
> agree   aim   appear   arrange   attempt
> can('t) afford   can't wait   decide   forget   hope
> intend   learn   manage   offer   plan   promise
> refuse   remember   seem   start   tend   try
>
> **Sometimes with an object**
> ask   beg   choose   dare   expect   help   need
> want   would like / love / hate / prefer
>
> **Always with an object**
> advise   allow   encourage   force   invite   order
> persuade   remind   teach   tell   warn (not)

Adjectives

You can use the infinitive after certain adjectives. These are usually adjectives expressing feelings, attitude, possibility, necessity or ability:
*I was so **surprised to see** Anna at the party.*
*Are you **ready to leave**?*

Here are some adjectives that can be followed by the infinitive.

> amazed   anxious   ashamed   careful   certain
> crazy   delighted   determined   difficult
> disappointed   easy   essential   fortunate   glad
> good   great   happy   important   (im)possible
> (un)likely   (un)lucky   necessary   normal
> pleased   proud   ready   reluctant   ridiculous
> sad   shocked   sorry   surprised   upset   willing

Nouns

You use the infinitive after certain nouns. These are usually nouns expressing feelings, attitude, possibility, necessity and ability:
*There's no **need to get** angry.*
*What's the best **way to get** to your house?*

Here are some nouns that can be followed by the infinitive.

> chance   decision   desire   idea   mistake
> need   opportunity   time   way

You can use the infinitive after certain nouns + a form of *be*:
*The **secret is to eat** healthily.*
*His **advice was to say** nothing.*
*The important **thing is to exercise** every day.*

Unit 4

Real and hypothetical situations

Conditional sentences have two clauses: an *if* clause and a main clause. The *if* clause can go at the beginning or the end of the sentence. When it comes at the beginning, it is followed by a comma (,). When it comes at the end, there is no comma separating the clauses:
If he works a bit harder, he should pass his exam.
He should pass his exam if he works a bit harder.

Real conditionals

Form

If	present tense	modal verb (*will /might*, etc) present tense imperative

The table shows the most common forms but other tenses and structures are also possible.
If + present + present is sometimes known as the 'zero conditional'.

If + present + modal (*will / might*, etc) is sometimes known as the 'first conditional'.

Use

The above forms refer to the present or future and express a real or possible situation:
*If you've got time, **will** you **help** me later?*
*If you **want** to be a pilot, then **do** it!*

You can use *If* + present + present when the main clause is seen as an automatic consequence of the *if* clause:
*Anything's possible if you **want** it enough.*

You can use *If* + present + modal when the main clause is a prediction, assumption, promise, or spontaneous decision, as a consequence of the *if* clause:
*If you **abandon** your dreams, you'll **regret** it forever.*

Unreal conditionals

Form

If	past tense	*would* + infinitive modal verb (*could / should*, etc)

If + past + *would* is sometimes known as the 'second conditional'.

Use

An unreal conditional also refers to the present or future and it expresses an unreal, hypothetical or extremely improbable situation:
*If you **had** unlimited talents and abilities, what **would** you **do**?*
*If I **spoke** better English, I **wouldn't need** to study.*

Wordlist

*** the 2,500 most common English words, ** very common words, * fairly common words

Unit 1

a bit of a clown *phrase* /ə ˌbɪt əv ə ˈklaʊn/
a bit of a loner *phrase* /ə ˌbɪt əv ə ˈləʊnə/
ambitious *adj* /æmˈbɪʃəs/ **
artistic *adj* /ɑːˈtɪstɪk/ **
assertive *adj* /əˈsɜːtɪv/
assertiveness *n* /əˈsɜːtɪvnəs/
be going to *v* /bi ˈgəʊɪŋ tə/
be meant to *phrase* /ˌbi ˈment tə/
be supposed to *phrase* /ˌbi səˈpəʊst tə/
boring *adj* /ˈbɔːrɪŋ/ **
calm *adj* /kɑːm/ **
can't bring (one)self to do (something)
   phrase /kɑːnt ˌbrɪŋ (wʌn)self tə ˈduː
   (sʌmθɪŋ)/
chat away *phrase* /tʃæt əˈweɪ/
creative *adj* /kriˈeɪtɪv/ **
dedication *n* /ˌdedɪˈkeɪʃn/ *
deep *adj* /diːp/ ***
dependable *adj* /dɪˈpendəbl/
dull *adj* /dʌl/ **
efficiency *n* /ɪˈfɪʃnsi/ **
efficient *adj* /ɪˈfɪʃnt/ ***
electronic organiser *n* /elekˌtrɒnɪk
   ˈɔːgənaɪzə/
energetic *adj* /enəˈdʒetɪk/ *
energy *n* /ˈenədʒi/ ***
entertaining *adj* /ˌentəˈteɪnɪŋ/ *
enthusiasm *n* /ɪnˈθjuːziˌæzəm/ **
enthusiastic *adj* /ɪnˌθjuːziˈæstɪk/ **
feel paranoid *phrase* /fiːl ˈpærəˌnɔɪd/
focused *adj* /ˈfəʊkəst/
give a good/bad/mixed impression *phrase*
   /gɪv ə ˌgʊd, bæd, mɪkst ɪmˈpreʃn/
go-getter *n* /ˈgəʊ ˌgetə/
impress *v* /ɪmˈpres/ **
impulsive *adj* /ɪmˈpʌlsɪv/
independent *adj* /ˌɪndɪˈpendənt/ ***
intend to *v* /ɪnˈtend tə/ ***
jot down *v* /dʒɒt ˈdaʊn/
leadership skills *n* /ˈliːdəʃɪp ˌskɪlz/
level-headed *adj* /ˌlevl ˈhedɪd/
lip balm *n* /ˈlɪp ˌbɑːm/
never leave home without (something)
   phrase /ˌnevə ˌliːv ˌhəʊm wɪˈðaʊt (sʌmθɪŋ)/
on your way to the top *phrase* /ˌɒn jə ˌweɪ
   tə ðə ˈtɒp/
over-confident *adj* /ˌəʊvəˈkɒnfɪdənt/
rational *adj* /ˈræʃn(ə)l/ **
rave about *v* /ˈreɪv əˌbaʊt/
self-confidence *n* /ˌself ˈkɒnfɪdəns/
self-confident *adj* /ˌself ˈkɒnfɪdənt/
self-sufficiency *n* /ˌselfsəˈfɪʃnsi/
self-sufficient *adj* /ˌselfsəˈfɪʃnt/
sense of style *n* /ˌsens əv ˈstaɪl/
spiritual *adj* /ˈspɪrɪtʃuəl/ **
submissive *adj* /səbˈmɪsɪv/
superficial *adj* /ˌsuːpəˈfɪʃl/ *
team-player *n* /ˈtiːm ˌpleɪə/
top executive material *phrase* /ˌtɒp
   ɪgˈzekjʊtɪv məˈtɪəriəl/
trot out *v* /trɒt ˈaʊt/
turn bright red *phrase* /ˌtɜːn ˌbraɪt ˈred/
turn out to be *phrase* /tɜːn ˌaʊt tə ˌbi/
well-balanced *adj* /ˌwel ˈbælənst/

Unit 2

a shoulder to cry on *phrase* /ə ˌʃəʊldə tə
   ˈkraɪ ɒn/
according to the survey *phrase* /əˌkɔːdɪŋ tə
   ðə ˈsɜːveɪ/
admit to *v* /ədˈmɪt tə/ ***
all but a handful *phrase* /ˌɔːl bət ə ˈhændfʊl/
amaze *v* /əˈmeɪz/ *
amusing *adj* /əˈmjuːzɪŋ/ *
annoy *v* /əˈnɔɪ/ **
at any one time *phrase* /ət ˌeni ˌwʌn ˈtaɪm/
be less likely to *phrase* /bi ˌles ˈlaɪkli tə/

be more likely to *phrase* /ˌbi ˌmɔː ˈlaɪkli tə/
be there for (someone) *v* /bi ˈðeə fə
   (sʌmwʌn)/
circle of friends *n* /ˌsɜːkl əv ˈfrendz/
companion *n* /kəmˈpænjən/ **
competitive *adj* /kəmˈpetətɪv/ **
confide in *v* /kənˈfaɪd ˌɪn/ *
cosmetic surgery *n* /kɒzˌmetɪk ˈsɜːdʒəri/
despite *prep* /dɪˈspaɪt/ ***
dominate *v* /ˈdɒmɪˌneɪt/ **
easy to talk to *adj* /ˌiːzi tə ˈtɔːk tuː/
easy-going *adj* /ˌiːziˈgəʊɪŋ/
fall out with (someone) *v* /ˌfɔːl ˈaʊt wɪð
   (sʌmwʌn)/
fall steadily *phrase* /fɔːl ˈstedəli/
fascinate *v* /ˈfæsɪneɪt/ *
full of (themselves) *phrase* /ˈfʊl əv
   (ðəmˌselvz)/
generous *v* /ˈdʒenərəs/ **
God's gift to women *v* /ˌgɒdz ˌgɪft tə ˈwɪmɪn/
have a tendency towards *phrase* /ˌhæv ə
   ˈtendənsi təˌwɔːdz/
in-crowd *n* /ˈɪnˌkraʊd/
interest *v* /ˈɪntrəst/ **
jealous *adj* /ˈdʒeləs/ *
keep a secret *phrase* /ˌkiːp ə ˈsiːkrət/
keep in touch *phrase* /ˌkiːp ɪn ˈtʌtʃ/
left-wing *adj* /ˌleft ˈwɪŋ/ *
looks *n* /lʊks/
lose touch *phrase* /ˌluːz ˈtʌtʃ/
more than half *phrase* /ˌmɔː ðən ˈhɑːf/
one in three *phrase* /ˌwʌn ɪn ˈθriː/
One thing I really (hate) *phrase* /wʌn ˌθɪŋ ˌaɪ
   ˌriːli (ˈheɪt)/
personality *n* /ˌpɜːsəˈnæləti/ ***
punctual *adj* /ˈpʌŋktʃuəl/
really good-looking *phrase* /ˌriːli ˌgʊd ˈlʊkɪŋ/
respect *n* /rɪˈspekt/ ***
right-wing *adj* /ˌraɪt ˈwɪŋ/ *
sense of humour *n* /ˌsens əv ˈhjuːmə/
six out of ten *phrase* /ˌsɪks ˌaʊt əv ˈten/
tend to *v* /ˈtend tə/ ***
the research identified *phrase* /ðə rɪˈsɜːtʃ
   aɪˌdentɪˌfaɪd/
the study revealed *phrase* /ðə ˈstʌdi rɪˌviːld/
the way (someone) dresses *phrase* /ðə ˌweɪ
   (sʌmwʌn) ˈdresɪz/
toned *adj* /təʊnd/
trustworthy *adj* /ˈtrʌstˌwɜːði/
turn to *v* /ˈtɜːn tə/
twice as much (time) *phrase* /ˌtwaɪs əz ˈmʌtʃ
   (taɪm)/
up top *phrase* /ˌʌp ˈtɒp/
What I really (can't stand) *phrase* /ˌwɒt ˌaɪ
   ˌriːli (kɑːnt ˈstænd)/
What really (irritates) me *phrase* /ˌwɒt ˌriːli
   (ˈɪrɪteɪts) mi/
whereas *conj* /weərˈæz/ ***
yet *conj* /jet/ ***

Unit 3

be overweight *phrase* /bi ˌəʊvəˈweɪt/
be reluctant to *phrase* /bi rɪˈlʌktənt tə/
be still going strong *phrase* /ˌbi ˌstɪl ˌgəʊɪŋ
   ˈstrɒŋ/
be willing to *phrase* /ˌbi ˈwɪlɪŋ tə/
be wrapped up in cotton wool *phrase* /ˌbi
   ˌræpt ˌʌp ɪn ˌkɒtn ˈwʊl/
charm *v* /tʃɑːm/ *
constantly *adv* /ˈkɒnstəntli/ **
due for release *phrase* /ˌdjuː fə rɪˈliːs/
early, mid- (twenties) *n* /ˌɜːli, ˌmɪd (ˈtwentiz)/
enter a talent show *phrase* /ˌentə ə ˈtælənt
   ʃəʊ/
get a tattoo *phrase* /ˌget ə tæˈtuː/
have a broken heart *phrase* /ˌhæv ə ˌbrəʊkn
   ˈhɑːt/
heavy drinking *phrase* /ˌhevi ˈdrɪŋkɪŋ/

in moderation *phrase* /ˌɪn ˌmɒdəˈreɪʃn/
in the genes *phrase* /ˌɪn ðə ˈdʒiːnz/
inner self *n* /ˌɪnə ˈself/
it's a good idea to *phrase* /ˌɪts ə ˌgʊd aɪˈdɪə
   tə/
it's a mistake to *phrase* /ˌɪts ə mɪˈsteɪk tə/
it's easy to *phrase* /ˌɪts ˈiːzi tə/
it's important to *phrase* /ˌɪts ɪmˈpɔːtənt tuː/
jaded *adj* /ˈdʒeɪdɪd/
keep (my) mind active *phrase* /ˌkiːp (maɪ)
   ˌmaɪnd ˈæktɪv/
knit *v* /nɪt/ **
(my) late (nineties) *phrase* /(maɪ) ˌleɪt
   (ˈnaɪntiz)/
live to a ripe old age *phrase* /ˌlɪv tuː ə ˌraɪp
   ˌəʊld ˈeɪdʒ/
loads of time(s) *phrase* /ˈləʊdz əv ˌtaɪm(z)/
longevity *n* /lɒnˈdʒevəti/
lyrics *n* /ˈlɪrɪks/ **
make your fortune *phrase* /ˌmeɪk jə ˈfɔːtjuːn/
middle age *n* /ˌmɪdl ˈeɪdʒ/
old age *n* /ˌəʊld ˈeɪdʒ/
people in high places *phrase* /ˌpiːpl ɪn ˌhaɪ
   ˈpleɪsɪz/
reference *n* /ˈref(ə)rəns/ ***
rub shoulders with *phrase* /ˌrʌb ˈʃəʊldəz wɪð/
sign up *v* /saɪn ˈʌp/
social class *n* /ˌsəʊʃl ˈklɑːs/
take oneself too seriously *phrase* /ˌteɪk
   wʌnˌself tuː ˈsɪəriəsli/
teens *n* /tiːnz/
the ups and downs of life (experience)
   phrase /ði ˌʌps ən ˌdaʊnz əv ˈlaɪf
   (ɪkˈspɪəriəns)/
try to *v* /ˈtraɪ tə/ ***

Unit 4

accomplish *v* /əˈkʌmplɪʃ/ *
beat (someone) down *v* /ˌbiːt (sʌmwʌn)
   ˈdaʊn/
bring (someone) up *v* /ˌbrɪŋ (sʌmwʌn) ˈʌp/
captivated *adj* /ˈkæptɪˌveɪtɪd/
chocolate taster *n* /ˈtʃɒklət ˌteɪstə/
crushed *adj* /krʌʃt/
degree *n* /dɪˈgriː/ ***
depressed *adj* /dɪˈprest/ **
downside *n* /ˈdaʊnˌsaɪd/
dream analyst *n* /ˈdriːm ˌænəlɪst/
exhilarated *adj* /ɪgˈzɪləˌreɪtɪd/
extreme explorer *n* /ɪkˌstriːm ɪkˈsplɔːrə/
follow your dream *phrase* /ˌfɒləʊ jə ˈdriːm/
forensic chemist *n* /fəˌrenzɪk ˈkemɪst/
give up *v* /gɪv ˈʌp/
go for *v* /ˈgəʊ fə/
go on to *v* /ˌgəʊ ˈɒn tə/
go up to *v* /ˌgəʊ ˈʌp tə/
grow up *v* /grəʊ ˈʌp/
humiliated *adj* /hjuːˈmɪliˌeɪtɪd/
hurricane hunter *n* /ˈhʌrɪkən ˌhʌntə/
kissing trainer *n* /ˈkɪsɪŋ ˌtreɪnə/
movie star *n* /ˈmuːvi ˌstɑː/
nightclub researcher *n* /ˈnaɪtklʌb rɪˌsɜːtʃə/
nine to five *phrase* /ˌnaɪn tə ˈfaɪv/
out of work *phrase* /ˌaʊt əv ˈwɜːk/
overtime *n* /ˈəʊvəˌtaɪm/ *
perks *n* /pɜːks/
regret *v* /rɪˈgret/ **
sack *v* /sæk/ **
scared *adj* /skeəd/ **
skateboard test rider *n* /ˈskeɪtbɔːd ˈtest
   ˌraɪdə/
supportive *adj* /səˈpɔːtɪv/
tester *n* /ˈtestə/
well-paid *adj* /ˌwel ˈpeɪd/

Communication activities

Unit 1, Reading and speaking Ex 1 page 4

Questionnaire analysis

You scored 13 points or more: You never take life too seriously. You're creative, enthusiastic and have a great sense of humour, although you need to be careful that you're not seen as a bit of a clown. You may be top of everybody's party list, but not necessarily top executive material.

You scored 9 to 12: No extremes for you – a well-balanced, rational, dependable person who friends turn to when they need good advice. Your aim in life is to keep a balance between work and leisure. You may not be aiming for the top, but you're a good team-player and you'll enjoy life whatever you do.

You scored 8 or fewer: You certainly are a go-getter. Nothing can stand in the way of you reaching the top. You're ambitious, focused and organised. You're assertive – you know what you want, and you know how to get it. But be careful – you may come across as over-confident and lose friends on your way to the top.

Unit 2, Language study Ex 4 page 8

Friendship survey	Me	____	____	____	____
1 Do you prefer friends of the same sex or opposite sex?					
2 How many close friends do you have? a Fewer than five. b Between five and ten. c More than ten.					
3 How long have you known your best friend? a Less than three years. b More than three years. c Since you were children.					
4 Do you know the colour of your best friend's eyes?	Y / N	Y / N	Y / N	Y / N	Y / N
5 Do you have any 'silent' friends who you keep in touch with mainly by email or text?	Y / N	Y / N	Y / N	Y / N	Y / N
6 Have you ever fallen out with a friend over a girlfriend or boyfriend?	Y / N	Y / N	Y / N	Y / N	Y / N
7 What is the most important quality of a friendship? a Being there for you. b Respect. c Fun and a sense of humour.					

1 Work in groups of five. Complete the first column yourself. Then write the name of the other people in your group at the top of each column. Ask them the questions and note down their answers.

2 Find a partner from another group. Combine your findings to make a total of ten people surveyed.

3 Write sentences about the findings of your survey.

Example:

> Women tend to prefer friends of both sexes, whereas men are more likely to choose other men as friends.
> Six out of ten said they knew the colour of their best friend's eyes.
> One in five admitted they have fallen out over a boyfriend or girlfriend.
> According to our study, most people feel that respect is the most important quality of a friendship.

Listening scripts

Unit 1 Making an impression

 Listening script 01

Reading text from page 2

 Listening script 02

energetic / energy   enthusiastic / enthusiasm
dependable / dependability
spiritual / spirituality   creative / creativity

 Listening script 03

1 Sarah Williams
The person who was interviewing me turned out to be a man whose car I'd hit in an accident outside my local supermarket about a year before. It was one of those silly accidents, caused by me eating a sandwich while I was driving. We swapped details and insurance stuff, and had a conversation. Even though it had all been my fault, he was nice enough. Anyway, I was really embarrassed during the whole interview while he had this look on his face like he couldn't quite remember who I was. At the end he asked me if we'd met before. I was going to tell him, but I just couldn't bring myself to do it and I just said, 'No, I don't think so.'

2 Alice Dixon
I was waiting with the others outside the interview room and by the time they called me, I'd been waiting for ages and they'd already interviewed three people. I'd been able to hear all the questions and answers through the door – all the questions were about current affairs. Because I was last and no-one could see me, I had my ear right up against the door for the third interview and I jotted down the questions and answers. When I went in, I was in such a flap because it was my first interview that I trotted out all the same answers even though the questions were different. They didn't actually say I was a liar, but they knew that I'd been listening in.

3 Robert McCrae
I had this really long interview. It was supposed to be with a man and a woman, but he'd been held up in traffic. About halfway through, as we were chatting away, he came in and at random asked me if I liked football. That was his one and only question. The woman was quite intense and scary, but I thought I was doing OK. Then, at the end I shook the bloke's hand, and totally failed to shake hers. I felt so paranoid about it that a fortnight later I wrote an email apologising. She wrote back saying the reason I didn't get the job wasn't because I hadn't shaken her hand, but because I was by far the worst candidate she had ever interviewed.

 Listening script 04

On his day off, I went to pick him up at the restaurant. When he finally appeared, I'd been waiting nervously for what seemed like an eternity … but then, in an instant, my dreams were shattered. He'd had his hair cut, blow-dried and gelled. It was so stiff you could crack an egg on it. He was wearing a purple nylon suit with the label still attached to the sleeve. It was meant to be the date of a lifetime, but my burning passion collapsed like a soufflé.

Unit 2 A shoulder to cry on

 Listening script 05

1 Toby talking about Jack
Important friendships? I think I'd say that I have a good mix of friends from different times in my life. I have six or seven close friends in the circle that Jack and I belong to. We meet when we can to catch up. It doesn't matter if we don't get in touch much, but we still know what everyone's doing. It's just not important to speak very often.

I've known Jack for 11 years, since I was 13. We became close for silly reasons really, like we found each other amusing. Actually, Jack makes everyone laugh. Now we share a flat in London and he's become one of my closest friends.

We're not actually that similar. Politically, we're miles apart. I'm quite left-wing and Jack's quite right-wing. He's a great competitor and I admire his competitive spirit. We don't share the same interest in sports – he's a runner, I'm a cricketer – but he's a real go-getter and I've got a lot of time for his attitude to life.

Jack's not exactly relaxing to be around, but he's a great listener. Trust is very important and I trust Jack. He and I have shared a lot of adventures together. We've been up mountains and in jungles, things like that.

I don't want to start a gender war, but I think that women use friends more for emotional things, and guys look for someone they can share an adventurous spirit with. It's fine if guys don't speak to each other for six months.

2 Jack talking about Toby
Toby and I were in school in Oxford from the age of 13, but we only got to know each other well when we were 16. We used to make each other laugh all the time – Toby's a really amusing guy. After school, I took a gap year and Toby went straight to university. But the following year Toby and I travelled in South America for six months. That was when we became really close.

Now that I share a flat with Toby, it's very easy to remain friends. It's important that the person you live with is a friend; you don't want hassle when you come home. Toby is really easy-going and never gives me a hard time about the flat. At home, we watch TV together, play computer games, that sort of thing. And we go out for drinks together.

Toby is very easy to talk to and we always have things to talk about. I don't feel he judges me, and I completely trust him – I think that's something very important. I don't have many secrets to tell, but I'll always confide in Toby, because I know he won't say anything to anyone. I would definitely go to Toby if I had a problem.

Have we had any arguments? I'm sure we've fallen out at times; when we were travelling, for example. Toby can be quite competitive at times. We sometimes argued about women – he's quite a jealous person, well, I suppose we both are, really. It's not easy when one of you meets a nice girl and the other doesn't. That is annoying, but I'd still like to go away with him again.

 Listening script 06

Reading text from page 7

 Listening script 07

(I = interviewer; V = Victoria; E = Emma; M = Marie; N = Nadine; L = Laura)
I: A recent survey suggests that women are not that different from men when it comes to picking a partner. We hit the streets of Bournemouth to see if it's true.

1 Victoria
I: Excuse me. We're doing a survey into what women look for in a partner. What do you think is important?
V: I like a guy to look a bit rugged with dark hair, blue eyes and a bit of stubble.
I: Mm, sounds like you know what you want.

2 Emma
I: Hi. We're doing a survey into what women look for in a partner. Could you tell me which you think is more important – looks or personality?
E: Er well, I'm usually attracted by looks to begin with, but a good personality is important. I mean, the one thing I can't stand is men who are really full of themselves – it puts me right off.
I: OK, thanks.

3 Marie
I: Hi there. We're doing a survey into what women look for in a partner – what's most important for you?
M: What I look for in a partner is warmth, intelligence, a good sense of humour … and a toned body! Oh, and a face like George Clooney.

4 Nadine
I: Hello, excuse me. We're doing a survey into what women look for in a partner. What do you think is more important – looks or personality?
N: I think personality is more important. It's no good if they're really good-looking but really annoying – you can't just sit and look at them all the time. What really annoys me is good-looking men who think they're God's gift to women.

5 Laura
I: Excuse me. We're doing a survey into what women look for in a partner – erm, what's more important for you – looks or personality?
L: Well, the first thing I notice about a man is the way he dresses. If he's really gorgeous, it doesn't matter what's up top, does it?
I: Thank you.

Unit 3 You're as old as you feel

 Listening script 08

(P = Presenter; J = Julian)
P: Welcome to *True Lives*. What is the recipe for a long life? Wouldn't we all like to know! Julian Brookes travelled last week to the French Pyrenees to visit Maurice Anasse, one of several people in his village who have lived to a hundred. So Julian, did you uncover the secret recipe for longevity?
J: Well, not exactly but I did learn a lot from meeting Maurice.
P: How old is he exactly?
J: Maurice is 102 and still going strong.
P: That's amazing. He must have seen the invention of all sorts of things we take for granted today.
J: That's right. He remembers seeing the first car in his village. He said that it went too fast and crashed.
P: Did he ever drive one of those early cars?
J: No, he never actually learnt to drive but he was the proud owner of a motorbike which he carried on riding until he was well into his eighties. He also used to love cycling and swimming – oh, and he particularly enjoyed dancing, especially the waltz. Now he gets his exercise taking his dog for a walk. He doesn't go far – just to the local café where he plays dominoes with his friends. He says it's playing dominoes that keeps his mind active.

P: Yes, I'm sure that's true. And are his friends as old as Maurice?

J: Not quite, but a couple of them are in their late nineties. And they all look after one another. If one of them doesn't turn up at the café, somebody goes to find out what's happened. It's like one big extended family.

P: How lovely. Now, how has Maurice managed to reach such a great age?

J: Well, Maurice says that if you want to live to a ripe old age, you need to keep moving, keep going forward and take every opportunity to do something new. For example, he started learning English when he was in his eighties and he got his first computer for his 100th birthday. He says he loves surfing the net.

P: Good for him. I don't suppose he drinks or smokes.

J: He drinks wine, but in moderation and he gave up smoking when he was 33.

P: Very wise. Perhaps the answer lies in the kind of work he did.

J: Well, he wanted to be a footballer, but his father wanted him to work in the family furniture-making business. So that's what he did until he retired at the age of 65.

P: So in fact there's nothing special about his lifestyle? Could it be in the genes?

J: Well, maybe. He has two younger brothers of 93 and 98. Scientists have examined him and they're desperate to find a genetic explanation. But Maurice has his own theory about the secret of his longevity.

P: Oh?

J: Yes, he says it has a lot to do with the inner self. He says his secret is to 'Live calmly, treat other people well and look forward to tomorrow'. He has such a positive outlook on life.

P: Well, he sounds like a really special person. I wonder what those scientists will find in his genes. Perhaps they're looking in the wrong place. I think it sounds as if Maurice's secret lies in his heart.

Listening script 09

Reading text from page 12

Listening script 10

Layla
I don't think there's an ideal age for getting married. I mean, it just depends, doesn't it? You can meet somebody and decide they're the one for you at any age. I know somebody who's 18 and she's getting married because she's *so* in love. I was like, 'Why don't you wait?' but she was like, 'I *so* know he's the man for me.'

Tom
I think around thirty is ideal, not before, because you want to have a life – go travelling, get a career and all that. But if you wait too long, you're getting a bit on the old side for starting a family.

Helen
As late as possible. I think the only reason for getting married is so that you've got company for your old age. I was forty-something and I've no regrets at all. I mean, I shudder to think who I might have married when I was young. It took me over forty years to decide what I wanted in a man – then I found him.

Elaine
Oh, 70. No, because at that age men are looking for someone to be a nurse. Let's see. I suppose 25 – you've had time to have a life, haven't you?

Leroy
You must be joking! I'm never getting married. Girls are really annoying. They just want you to work and work and give them all the money to buy stupid things like make-up and clothes and 'Oh, darling, I need a pair of shoes' when they've already got 100 pairs of shoes. No way!

Unit 4 A dream job

Listening script 11

Reading text from page 15

Listening script 12

(I = Interviewer; G = George; R = Ronnie; L = Lou)

1 George
I: George, your job sounds too good to be true. How did you end up here?

G: I started as an analytical chemist and worked my way up to the top.

I: So, what qualifications do you need?

G: You need a degree in science or maths and ten or more years' experience in a food-related industry.

I: And apart from qualifications, do you have any special skills?

G: Oh yes – the ability to taste and a good sense of smell.

I: Why are you suited to this kind of work?

G: I'm always curious about 'what makes things tick' and I have an analytical approach to problem-solving.

I: What's the best thing about your work?

G: Working for a business where the purpose is to give people pleasure. And the job has its perks – I can eat as much chocolate as I like and I don't have to pay for it.

I: And the worst things?

G: Administrative paperwork.

I: Any advice for someone who wants to work in this field?

G: Concentrate on maths at school and be willing to try every food you come across.

2 Ronnie
I: Ronnie, you have an extraordinary job. Can you explain how you got it?

R: Yeah. Actually, it was through somebody I know. She was working for a film company and they were doing a romantic comedy, so obviously there was a lot of kissing. Erm, and the original kissing trainer kept turning up late, so he was sacked. They had to get a replacement very quickly, so my friend got me the job.

I: But do you need any special qualifications?

R: Yes, I have a degree in sociology and I specialised in the meaning of body language.

I: What exactly does your job involve?

R: I have to train actors to kiss properly. What you see on screen takes hours of practice.

I: What's the best thing about your job?

R: Kissing top actresses and getting paid to do it! No, seriously, I love working with a group of people towards a common cause. I guess I'm what you would call a team-player.

I: Are there any downsides to your job?

R: We have to work very long hours on film sets. I don't mind doing overtime, but my girlfriend isn't too happy about it.

3 Lou
I: Lou, your job sounds amazing. How did you get it?

L: It was a competition for all jobless under 25s. At the time I was out of work, so I entered and I was chosen. I was the right person for the job.

I: What qualifications and skills do you need?

L: Well, first of all, I'm a traveller at heart – I spent six months backpacking around Asia and Latin America. And of course I'm a party animal! Basically, I love travelling, and I love going out dancing.

I: Right. So what exactly do you do?

L: I go clubbing every night! I travel round the world, finding the best clubs of the moment. Then I send my report to my magazine and they print it every month.

I: What do you enjoy most about your job?

L: Oh, where do I start? I don't work nine to five, yippee! I meet lots of interesting people, see so many awesome places, and I spend my time doing what I love – dancing and socialising. Oh, and it's well paid, too.

I: Is there anything you don't like about your job?

L: Erm, it might sound strange, but sometimes I wake up and I don't know what continent I'm in, let alone which city I'm in. Oh, and I hate typing my reports, but I have to send them by email.

Unit 5 Review

Listening script 13

Part 1
(MJ1 = male judge 1; MJ2 = male judge 2; FJ = female judge)

MJ1: Well, congratulations to the three finalists. They are all talented singers and clearly popular with the general public, but we have to choose just one of them to win the title *Teen idol* and the recording contract. So, let's get started. What do you think of Sam?

MJ2: Sam is a very creative person. He can turn an average song into a work of art.

FJ: Yes, and he's so entertaining and energetic. Everyone loves his sense of humour.

MJ1: OK, yes, he's enthusiastic and he can be entertaining but just because he's a bit of a clown it doesn't make him a teen idol. … Come on, I just don't think that a sense of humour is the key to stardom and I think it's time to get real and judge him on his singing talents.

FJ: OK, I agree but I do think he's a talented performer, too. He's got a fantastic voice.

MJ1: All right, we'll come back to Sam. What about Lisa?

MJ2: I have to say that I find Lisa rather dull. It's just that I find it hard to really believe in her when she sings.

FJ: I think that's really unfair. She's got a great voice and she gets on so well with the other contestants. She's the number one team-player in my opinion.

MJ1: Let's not get carried away here. I agree with Jim. I think she comes across as a bit superficial. OK, she's dependable – you know that she will always deliver a decent song, but she doesn't have star quality.

FJ: Have you got anything good to say about Camellia or are you going to be negative about her as well?

MJ1: Well, Camellia is ambitious …

MJ2: Maybe a little bit too ambitious …

MJ1: Well maybe, but you need to be a go-getter in this game and you need to be self-confident in order to survive.

FJ: Well, I think she's brilliant. Her voice is rich and soulful and her self-confidence comes through clearly.

MJ1: I agree. Throughout this competition she's remained level-headed. For me she shows star quality while keeping her feet firmly on the ground.

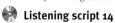 Listening script 14

Part 2
MJ1: … so after considering our decision very carefully, we declare the winner of *Teen idol* the amazing talents of … Camellia!

 Listening script 15

Song from page 21

Communication activities

Unit 3, Speaking Ex 3 page 13

▲ Layla, 17　　　▲ Tom, 27　　　▲ Helen, 54　　　▲ Elaine, 77　　　▲ Leroy, 13

Unit 4, Writing Ex 2 page 17

CURRICULUM VITAE

PERSONAL DETAILS

Name: Elizabeth Jones

Date of Birth: 9th February 1985

Address: 13, Spencer Rd, Oxford

Telephone: 01865 1324576

Sex: Female

Marital Status: Single

Nationality: English

-O-O-O-O-O-O-O-O-O-O-O-O-O-O-O-O-O-O-O-O-O-O-O-O-O-O-O-O-O-

Skills

Word-processing skills

French

Driving licence (2 speeding fines)

Education

1993–1997 Spencer Road Junior School

1997–2004 Isis High: 10 GCSEs and 3 A levels – English, French, Biology, (failed Geography)

2004–2007 Bath University: BA in English

Work history

2004–2005: Bar Manager at the Metro Bar, Bath

I became familiar with the full range of products supplied in the bar and enjoyed striking up a rapport with customers. (Left after disagreement with the owner.)

Hobbies and interests

Captain of the University Women's Basketball Club

Taking my two dogs (Wolfie and Bear) for walks

Travelling, Salsa

References

Mr Derek Jones 13, Spencer Road

Module 2
Things

Unit	Topic	Language study	Vocabulary	Main skills
1 **Food for thought** pages 34–37	• Mood food (A person's relationship with food) • Fred's phone-in (Advice from a nutritionist) • What's your food IQ? (A nutrition quiz)	• Indirect questions	• Food • Taste and texture	• **Reading:** identifying the writer • **Speaking:** discussing food and eating habits; discussing nutrition and health • **Listening:** identifying key information
2 **State of the art** pages 38–41	• Mobile phone mania • Techno tales (News stories about technology)	• Types of phrasal verbs	• Expressions with *make* and *do* • Gadgets • Discussion phrases	• **Reading:** checking facts; summarising • **Speaking:** discussing mobile phone use and gadgets; using discussion phrases • **Listening:** predicting and comparing • **Pronunciation:** sentence stress and intonation
3 **Money talks** pages 42–45	• I sold my first car by 11 and earned a million by 14 • Attitudes to money	• Talking about the present (present simple, present continuous, present perfect, *will*)	• Verbs to talk about money • Expressions to talk about money	• **Pronunciation:** vowel sounds • **Reading:** choosing a summary; identifying key information; understanding vocabulary in context • **Listening:** understanding main points and identifying key information • **Speaking:** discussing attitudes to money
4 **I could kick myself** pages 46–49	• What's in a name? (Problems with brand naming) • Music and advertising	• Unreal past and regrets	• Advertising and branding • Expressions for memories and associations	• **Reading:** identifying key information; understanding paragraph topics; understanding vocabulary in context • **Listening:** predicting and checking; listening for key language • **Speaking:** discussing successful brand names; talking about memories and associations • **Writing:** a letter of complaint

1 Food for thought

Mood food

Lead-in **1** Work with a partner. Look at the photos of food. Which of the items are you more likely to eat when you are:

a bored   b tired   c down   d happy   e ill?

Reading and vocabulary **1** 🎧 **16** Read the magazine article on page 35. Which of the food items in the photos is not mentioned?

2 Do you think the text was written by a man or a woman? Why?

3 Put the words in the box into the correct group. Which words do you think are negative?

crusty bland gooey mild greasy chewy creamy sour tangy sickly crunchy tender sweet tough buttery spicy soggy crisp savoury juicy salty hot

Texture	**Taste**
crusty	*buttery*

4 Work with a partner and <u>underline</u> the food items in the text. Then choose six items and describe their taste and texture using the words in Ex 3.

Example: *cheese – creamy, greasy, buttery, tangy, bland, mild, savoury*

5 Describe the taste and texture of your favourite dish and a dish you can't stand.

For me, food isn't about hunger, it's about *my moods*

When I'm bored, I poke around in the fridge, eat a slice of cheese maybe, or a tomato, or a carrot – peeled and nibbled from the outside inwards, so I end up with the fragile central core.

When I'm tired, I eat roasted peppers, creamy rice pudding, shortbread biscuits dunked in sweet tea.

When I'm a bit low, I eat chocolate, letting it melt in my mouth.

When I feel anxious, I make cakes or biscuits, even in the middle of the night, and the smell of baking reassures me: ginger biscuits, tangy lemon tart, chocolate cake.

When I'm in a good mood, I wake in the early hours and plan meals for guests (salmon with lime, pear and almond tart, strawberries, passion fruit, great gooey wheels of brie), and it's like thinking about Christmas presents.

When work is going well, I will often cook slow, satisfying meals: soups, crusty pies, things that rise in the oven if I'm lucky. There's something very comforting about a pot simmering on the stove, life running according to plan.

In the morning I don't like breakfast, because food for me is like some kind of a reward: eating straight after sleeping treats food as fuel.

I love eating late: food as a treat at the end of the day. Snacks in bed are bliss: a boiled egg with buttered toast and crumbs in the sheets.

When I'm excited, I rarely feel hungry, for then I want to be light-footed and empty – a piece of steamed fish, maybe, or a green salad; something clean and light that won't weigh me down; sushi is perfect.

When I'm guilty or agitated, I push things round my plate. When I'm sad, I starve myself.

'Mood food' by Nicci Gerrard for *The Observer Magazine*

Speaking **1** Work in small groups and discuss these questions.

1 What's your favourite:
  a snack
  b comfort food
  c meal of the day
  d restaurant and dish on the menu
  e childhood memory food?

2 Do you usually:
  a eat fast
  b eat slowly
  c push the food round the plate
  d eat the best bits first or keep the best till last?

2 What's the best meal you've ever had and the worst meal you've ever had?

Fred's phone-in

Listening **1** What kind of benefits / problems can you get by eating the right / wrong sort of food?

Example: *more energy from the right food, weight problems from the wrong food*

2 🔘 **17** Listen to the phone-in to a nutrition expert and choose the correct alternative.

1 Caller 1 a is a bad student.
          b is nervous in exams.
          c has lost his memory.

2 Caller 2 a has a problem with her mother.
          b is allergic to fast food.
          c has got spotty skin.

3 Caller 3 a is angry with her brother.
          b has an angry brother.
          c is allergic to her brother.

3 Work with a partner. What's the expert's advice to each caller? Listen again and check.

LANGUAGE STUDY

Indirect questions

1 Compare the indirect questions from the phone-in with the direct questions. Answer questions 1–3.

Direct question	Indirect question
Is there anything I can eat that will boost my memory?	*I was wondering if there was anything I could eat that would boost my memory?*
How much fresh fruit and vegetables do you eat?	*Could you tell me how much fresh fruit and vegetables you eat?*
What can I give my brother for his fiery temper?	*I'd like to know what I can give my brother for his fiery temper?*

1 Which type of question is more tentative, formal or polite?

2 How is the structure of the indirect questions different from the direct questions? Think about the use of introductory phrases, tenses, the auxiliary verb *do* and word order.

3 Which word is used instead of a question word in *yes /no* questions?

Grammar reference page 58

2 These questions are from later in the phone-in. Write the second part of the questions in the correct order.

1 Could you tell me   drink / how much / water / I / each day / should / ?
2 Do you know   there / if / to help me sleep better / is / anything I can eat / ?
3 Have you any idea   the most nutritious / is / which food / ?
4 I just wanted to know   comes / the best wine / where / from / ?
5 Would you say   healthier / a vegetarian diet / for you / is / ?
6 I was wondering   is / what / for healthy hair / to eat / the best thing /?

3 Can you answer any of the questions in Ex 2?

4 Work with a partner. Each think of a subject that you know a lot about or choose an idea from the box. Prepare some questions about your partner's subject using the introductory phrases in Ex 2.

> food   drink   cooking   a type of music   the USA   a sport   fashion
> business   transport   cinema   television   computers
> the history of your country

5 Work with a partner. Ask and answer each other's questions and find out as much information as you can. Who would make the best radio phone-in expert?

6 For more personal questions we can use *Do you mind if I ask you …?* Change these direct questions into indirect questions beginning with *Do you mind if I ask you …?*

Example: How old are you? *Do you mind if I ask you how old you are?*

1 Which political party do you vote for?
2 Have you got any tattoos?
3 What's your natural hair colour?
4 How many girl / boyfriends have you had?
5 How much did your watch cost?
6 Where did you get your shoes?
7 Do you snore?

7 Work with a partner. Ask and answer the questions in Ex 6. If you feel the question is too personal, you can use these expressions.

1 Neutral refusal: I'd rather not answer that.
2 Informal refusal: Don't be so nosey!

What's your food IQ?

Reading and speaking   **1**   Look at the nutrition quiz and answer the questions.

How health conscious are you?

How much do you know about the food that you eat? For example, did you know that a large milkshake has more calories than three cheeseburgers? No? Well, you'd better take our quiz and test your nutrition knowledge.

1   Which contains the most fat?
   a   a packet of crisps
   b   a cereal bar
   c   a bar of chocolate

2   How many teaspoons of sugar are there in the average can of cola?
   a   2–4   **b**   5–7   **c**   more than 7

3   How many calories are there in the average bottle of beer?
   a   100   **b**   250   **c**   500

4   Which of the following burns the most calories?
   a   weight training   **b**   yoga   **c**   walking

5   If you feel tired, weak and pale, you should eat foods containing more:
   a   vitamins   **b**   iron   **c**   calcium

6   Which of the following has the highest concentration of vitamin C?
   a   carrots   **b**   potatoes   **c**   broccoli

7   Which of the following is generally worse for your skin?
   a   smoking
   b   drinking alcohol
   c   eating sweets

8   In a healthy adult, what proportion of the body should be fat?
   a   male 10–15%, female 20–25%
   b   female 10–15%, male 20–25%
   c   male and female 15–20%

9   Which of the following is it best to avoid if you want to lose weight?
   a   biscuits   **b**   bread   **c**   chips

10   Which are more nutritious: fresh fruit and vegetables or frozen fruit and vegetables?
   a   fresh   **b**   frozen   **c**   there's no difference

Turn to page 61 for the answers. Give yourself 1 point for each correct answer.

WHAT IT MEANS

0–4   Hello? How have you survived this long?
5–7   Plenty of room for improvement.
8–10   Well done, you healthy specimen.

2   Compare your results with other students in the class. Were there any answers that surprised you?

3   Think about your answers to these questions. Work in small groups and discuss your ideas.
   1   Generally speaking, do you think people in your country have a healthy diet?
   2   Which country do you think has the healthiest diet? Why?
   3   Which foreign foods have you tried? Which is your favourite?

CD-ROM   For more activities go to **Things Unit 1**

2 State of the art

	LEARNING AIMS
	• Can use different types of phrasal verbs
	• Can use expressions with *make* and *do*
	• Can discuss technology

Lead-in   **1**   Work with a partner. How would life be different without mobile phones? Discuss your ideas.

2   Look at the mobile phone quiz and answer the questions.

How much do you **know about mobiles?**

1   The first person to make a mobile phone call was
   a Mr Nokia   **b** Mr Motorola   **c** Mr Ericsson

2   The Motorola company launched their first ever mobile phone in Europe in
   a the late 70s   **b** the early 80s   **c** the mid-80s

3   Early phones were heavy because they contained
   a Wind up mechanisms   **b** A large battery
   c A generator

4   For the mobile companies, introducing text messaging was
   a low priority   **b** top priority
   c equal priority with phoning

5   The first cross-network text message was sent in
   a 1988   **b** 1998   **c** 2001

6   The mobile phone number worth the most money is
   a 88888   **b** 12345   **c** 01010

Reading   **1**   **18**   Read the text and check your answers to Lead-in Ex 2.

'Mobile phone mania' by Ashley Norris for *Britannia in flight magazine*

Mobile phone **mania**

One day, back in 1910, Lars Magnus Ericsson and his wife set off for a drive in the Swedish countryside. They were miles from the nearest town when they ran into trouble and had to make an urgent phone call. Improvising with long sticks, they made a connection through telephone wires and were soon chatting to the operator. They had made the first ever mobile phone call.

Today, Ericsson, albeit after doing a deal with Japanese electronic giant Sony, is one of the biggest mobile phone makers in the world.

Believe it or not, it was only in the mid-1980s that Motorola brought out their first ever mobile in Europe. The brick-sized handsets came with a huge battery. When these models first came out, few people could afford them, so they were largely bought by high-flying executives, who could continue to do business as they travelled.

Mobile phones really came of age in the 1990s when prices came down and they became the must-have gadget for everyone from salespeople to teenagers.

Mobile phone business analyst Jamie Strachan cites two major reasons for their growth. 'First, the handsets became digital, ensuring much better sound quality and coverage. The new digital models are also smaller and cheaper. Second, SMS (short messaging service) or "texting" as it has become known, captured the imagination of the public.'

It might seem strange but texting was such a low priority for the networks that it took several years before people using one network could pick up a message from someone using another. When cross-network messaging was implemented in 1998, the phone companies suddenly found they were struggling to keep up with the demand for texting.

Mobile phone numbers are notoriously unmemorable, but networks have been making money charging a fortune for special numbers. One man made an offer of £15,000 for the number 0700 123 456, but the network who owns it has turned the bid down. It says that it's looking for offers in excess of £50,000.

The most valuable number of all is 88888. Eight is a lucky number in China and Chinese businessmen have reportedly been contacting telecom companies offering thousands of pounds to snap it up.

As picture messaging and video calling become mainstream, no one is quite sure what the mobile phone companies will come up with next. But whatever happens, old Mr Ericsson would certainly be amazed at what his drive in the countryside has started.

2 Work with a partner. Put this summary of the text in the correct order.

a   introduced, they had trouble keeping up with demand. People will pay huge sums ☐

b   until the mid-1980s that mobile phones went on sale in Europe. Early ☐

c   handsets transformed the industry and everybody wanted one. At first, texting ☐

d   Lars Ericsson improvised the first mobile phone call in 1910 but it wasn't **1**

e   was low priority for phone companies, but when cross-network messaging was ☐

f   of money for lucky or memorable phone numbers. As video calling becomes ☐

g   mainstream, who knows what phone companies will come up with next? ☐

h   models were too heavy and expensive for most people, but in the 90s digital ☐

make and *do*

Vocabulary   **1**   Do these words form expressions with *make* or *do*? Check your answers in the text.

1   a phone call   3   a deal   5   money

2   a connection   4   business   6   an offer

make	*do*
a phone call	

2   Copy the table. Put the words and phrases into the correct group.

someone a favour   an important decision   an exam   a mess of something
a big mistake   some damage   a list   a good / bad impression
some exercise   a new friend   a course   a complaint   a lot of effort
a lot of work   a fuss about something   your best

3   Work with a partner. Tell each other about a time when you did or are going to do some of the things in Ex 2. Find out as much information as you can.

Speaking   **1**   Work with a partner. Read these statistics and discuss the questions.

- 80% of 15 to 24-year-olds in the UK use texting to organise their social lives.
- 40% of the UK population use it to quietly say 'I love you'.
- 13% have used texting to end relationships.

1   Are you surprised by the statistics?

2   Have you done any of the things listed?

3   What do you use your mobile phone for?

2   Which of these gadgets do you use? Which could you not live without?

computer games console

iPod

watch

hairdryer

DVD player

digital camera

mobile

LANGUAGE STUDY

Types of phrasal verbs

1 Look at these sentences about the text. Match the phrasal verbs in **bold** to each of the four types in the table.

a   *Lars Magnus Ericsson and his wife* **set off** *for a drive in the Swedish countryside.* ☐

b   *They were miles from the nearest town when they* **ran into trouble**. ☐

c   *The most valuable number of all is 88888. Chinese businessmen have been offering thousands of pounds to* **snap it up**. ☐

d   *The mobile phone companies will need to* **come up with** *new gimmicks.* ☐

2-part verbs		
Type 1:	Does not take an object.	*My car* **broke down** *the other day.*
Type 2:	Must have an object.	*Can you* **turn off the TV?**
	Can be separated by the object.	*Can you* **turn the TV off?**
	Must be separated when the object is a pronoun.	*Can you* **turn it off?** Not: ~~*Can you* **turn off it?**~~
Type 3:	Must have an object. Can't be separated by the object.	*I'll* **look through the manual.** *I'll* **look through it.**
3-part verbs		
Type 4:	Must have an object. Can't be separated by the object.	*The printer's* **run out of ink.**

Grammar reference page 58

2 Which type (1, 2, 3 or 4) is each of the phrasal verbs in *italics*?
1   I never go to the cinema to see films. I wait until they *bring* them *out* on DVD.
2   I'll get a TV-mobile phone when the price *comes down* a little.
3   There's a song I really want to find. I've spent ages *looking for* it on the internet.
4   I've been sent some important emails, so I need to *pick* them *up* after the lesson.
5   I'm happy with my old mobile. I'm not bothered about *keeping up with* the latest models.
6   I bought a picture-messaging phone as soon as they *came out*.
7   Even if I was offered a fortune to work in a telephone call centre, I'd still *turn it down*.
8   I've had my computer for ages, but I've never played any of the games that *came with* it.

3 What is the meaning of each of the phrasal verbs in Ex 2? Which of the statements are true for you?

4 Write the objects in brackets in the correct place in these sentences. Use the information in the box to help you.
1   Sorry, I think I pressed something by mistake and *cut off*. (us)
2   You're busy now? OK, I'll *call back* later. (you)
3   My brother is always using the phone. I wish he'd *get off* once in a while. (it)
4   I need to *look up* in the phone directory. (their number)
5   I've *run out of* on my mobile so I need to *top up*. (credit, it)
6   I need to *get through to*, but I can't *get hold of*. (my sister, her)

Type 2: cut off, call back, look up, top up

Type 3: get off

Type 4: run out of, get through to, get hold of

5 Match the phrasal verbs in *italics* in Ex 4 with the definitions in the box.

> buy more credit   call again   contact   disconnected   find
> stop using   used all (the)   speak to

6 Work with a partner. Student A turn to page 61. Student B turn to page 64.

Techno tales

Listening **1** Work with a partner. Look at these headlines which all relate to news about technology. Discuss what you think each story is about.

Computer love

Changing shape of the thumb

Adverts on the moon

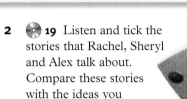

Pilotless passenger planes

Staying young is in the jeans

2  **19** Listen and tick the stories that Rachel, Sheryl and Alex talk about. Compare these stories with the ideas you discussed in Ex 1.

3 All of the stories in Ex 2 were actually reported, but one of them was a hoax. Which do you think it was? Check your answers on page 64.

Discussion phrases

Pronunciation and speaking **1** Complete these sentences with the words in the box using the meanings in brackets to help you. Then listen again and check your answers.

| way wrong Apparently surprise kidding Actually off |
| mean Basically |

1 You're _____! (You're joking!)

2 Well, it wouldn't _____ me. (I can believe that.)

3 What do you _____? (I don't understand.)

4 _____, they've brought out jeans that keep you young. (someone said)

5 No _____! (Really?)

6 _____, you just have to wear these jeans. (essentially)

7 Come _____ it! (I don't believe it.)

8 I might be _____, but … (I'm not sure, but …)

9 _____, I think it's a brilliant idea. (on the contrary)

2 **20** Listen and repeat the sentences. Pay attention to stress and intonation.

3 Work in groups and choose one of the topics in the box. Discuss the topics using the phrases in Ex 1. The first person to use all the phrases is the winner.

| pilotless planes living longer cloning clothes of the future the internet |
| marriage extreme sports space travel too much technology best job |

 **CD-ROM** For more activities go to **Things Unit 2**

3 Money talks

Lead-in   **1**   They say, 'Money can't buy you happiness'. Do you agree?

Vocabulary and pronunciation

1   The verbs in the box are used to talk about money. Put them into groups: positive, negative or neutral. Then compare your ideas with a partner.

Example: positive – *earn*

> burn   r<u>ai</u>se   donate   <u>ea</u>rn   f<u>a</u>ke   inv<u>e</u>st   l<u>ea</u>ve   l<u>e</u>nd   l<u>o</u>se   rec<u>ei</u>ve   s<u>a</u>ve
> sp<u>e</u>nd   w<u>a</u>ste   w<u>i</u>n   st<u>ea</u>l

2   Match the verbs in Ex 1 to these vowel sounds.

   1   /eɪ/   4   /iː/
   2   /ɪ/   5   /e/
   3   /ɜː/   6   /uː/

   Example: /e/ – *spend*

3   🔘 **21**   Complete the poem with some of the verbs in Ex 1. Think about rhyming sounds. Then listen and check your answers.

4   Work with a partner. Use some of the verbs in Ex 1 to talk about yourself or people you know.

   Example: *My cousin won five hundred euros in a competition last year.*

Money

Workers (1) _____ it,
Spendthrifts burn it,
Bankers lend it,
Women (2) _____ it,
Forgers (3) _____ it,
Taxes take it,
Dying (4) _____ it,
Heirs receive it,
Thrifty (5) _____ it,
Misers crave it,
Robbers seize it,
Rich increase it,
Gamblers (6) _____ it,
I could use it.

Reading   **1**   What qualities do you think you need to become a millionaire?

2   🔘 **22**   Read the article about Tom Hartley on page 43 and choose the best summary of the key to his success.

   a   He was born into a wealthy family and enjoys life's luxuries.
   b   He's no different from the average man in the street. He's just been very lucky.
   c   He works very hard and has a strong desire to achieve.

3   Are these statements true or false?

   1   When Tom was 11, his father was a car dealer. ☐

   2   Tom left school early but continued his education with a private tutor. ☐

   3   When he was 14, Tom inherited £1 million. ☐

   4   Tom meets people from all walks of life in his job. ☐

   5   Tom has an extravagant lifestyle. ☐

   6   Tom thinks good business sense is something you are born with, not something you learn. ☐

4   Read the text again and check your answers.

I sold my first car at 11 and earned a million by 14

All my life, I've been around cars. Some of my earliest memories are of being in the showroom and watching my father close deals for cars such as Ferraris and Lamborghinis. I left school early, but I was learning the same things that were on the school curriculum – maths from working out deals, science from understanding how cars worked, and geography from travelling the country to buy cars worth up to £1 million.

Everyone's good at something: I discovered my forte at an early age, and was fortunate enough to have a father who was already in the car business. I sold my first car – a Porsche convertible – at the age of 11 and by the time I was 14, I was buying and selling around three cars a week. That was the age I became Britain's youngest self-made millionaire.

Sometimes people make the mistake of thinking that success has been handed to me on a plate. But everything I have I've earned myself – and all my share of the profits went into a trust fund so that at 18 I was able to buy half the business. Since then, I've continued to build on the company's success and feel very fortunate to be involved in something I enjoy so much. I love the fact that I get to meet different kinds of people through my work. One day I'll be dealing with the guy from the corner shop who's buying a Mercedes for his wife, and the next I'll be meeting somebody famous.

I have a comfortable life, but it's not overly ostentatious. I don't have a car of my own. When I get to work, I'll drive whatever car happens to be on the forecourt, and most days I'll roll up my sleeves and wash it too. I haven't had a proper holiday for years and I still live in the family home. I'm having my own house built at the moment and my fiancée and I will move in after we get married.

In my opinion, natural business acumen is not something that can be taught – it comes from inside. There has to be an inherent competitive streak. Good salesmen are in competition with themselves – they're always striving to do better and sell more. They set themselves clear goals, and stick to them. They don't waste time on negativity and worrying about things that might never happen.

'I sold my car at 11 and earned a million by 14' by Tom Hartley Jnr for the *Daily Mail*

Vocabulary

1 Replace the underlined words with words and phrases from the text. Make any necessary changes.

1 Academic achievement is not necessarily their <u>greatest strength</u>. (line 11)
2 They work very hard. Success is not <u>made easy for them</u>. (line 19)
3 They choose a lifestyle that is not <u>too extravagant</u>. (line 32)
4 They have <u>inborn business sense</u>. (line 40)
5 They have an innate <u>desire to be number one</u>. (line 42)
6 They <u>decide on their aims</u> and work very hard to achieve them. (line 45)

2 The statements in Ex 1 describe what you need to become a millionaire according to a book called *Think Yourself Rich*. Do you know any people who fit these descriptions?

LANGUAGE STUDY

Talking about the present

1   Look at these extracts from the text. Match the verbs in **bold** to the uses a–f.

   1   *Everything I have I've **earned** myself.*
   2   *Good salesmen **are** in competition with themselves.*
   3   *I **get** to meet different kinds of people through my work.*
   4   *I'm **having** my own house built at the moment.*
   5   *Since I was 18, I've **continued** to build on the company's success.*
   6   *I **feel** very fortunate to be involved in something I **enjoy** so much.*

Present simple	a	for something that is seen as true in general ☐2
	b	for something that happens all the time or repeatedly ☐
	c	for a state (such as feelings, likes, senses, etc) ☐
Present continuous	d	for something temporary and in progress ☐
Present perfect	e	for something that happened in the past and has a consequence now ☐
	f	for something that started in the past and continues now ☐

Grammar reference page 58

2   Complete these facts about the dollar with the correct form of the verbs.

   1   The word *dollar* (come) _____ from 'thaler', a 16th-century Bohemian coin.
   2   The dollar (be) _____ the official currency of the USA since 1785.
   3   On average, each one-dollar bill (have) _____ a life of about five years.
   4   It is estimated that $1000 billion in cash (circulate) _____ worldwide. The FBI (believe) _____ that up to $1 billion of this is counterfeit.
   5   Each day, the Bureau of Engraving and Printing (produce) _____ 37 million notes.
   6   The words 'In God We Trust' (be) _____ on all US currency since 1963.
   7   Martha Washington is the only woman who (ever / appear) _____ on a US note.

3   One of the facts in Ex 2 is not true. Which do you think it is?

4   Work with a partner. How much do you know about your country's currency? Discuss its history, different coins and notes and any other facts you know.

will

5   Look at this extract from the text and answer the question.

*When I get to work, I'll **drive** whatever car happens to be on the forecourt and most days I'll **roll up** my sleeves and wash it too.*

Is *will* used:
a   to refer just to the future?   b   to express a predictable habit?

Grammar reference page 59

6   Complete these sentences so that they are true for you.

Example: *Most weekends, I'll meet my friends for a drink.*

   1   Most weekends, I'll ...
   2   From time to time, I'll ...
   3   For lunch, I'll usually ...
   4   In the evenings, I'll generally ...
   5   If ever I'm bored, I'll usually ...
   6   If I can, I'll always ...

Listening and speaking 1 🔘 **23** A magazine is running a feature called 'Attitudes to money across the generations'. Listen to the interview with Joan, Sally and Nell and answer these questions.

Who:
1 spends most of her money on food?
2 doesn't have a credit card?
3 would spend lottery money on designer clothes?

▲ Joan   ▲ Sally   ▲ Nell

2 Match the <u>underlined</u> expressions from the interview to the definitions.

Name		
_____	1 She's <u>in the red</u>.	a short of money
_____	2 She <u>finds it hard to make ends meet</u>.	b buys herself something nice
_____	3 She's always <u>broke</u>.	c rich
_____	4 She thinks people should have <u>money put by for a rainy day</u>.	d overdrawn
_____		e doesn't have enough money to live on
_____	5 She <u>treats herself</u> occasionally	f savings
_____	6 She's going to be <u>loaded</u>.	g spend extravagantly
_____	7 She'd <u>splash out on</u> a world cruise.	

3 Who do the <u>underlined</u> expressions in Ex 2 refer to? Listen to the interview again and write the correct name next to 1–7.

4 Whose attitude is most like your own attitude to money?

5 Think about your answers to these questions. Then think about how your parents and grandparents would answer them. Work with a partner and discuss your ideas.

1 What do you spend most money on?
2 Are you a saver or a spender?
3 What is your biggest money weakness?
4 Do you prefer cash or credit cards?
5 Have you ever won or surprisingly come into a sum of money?
6 When was the last time you splashed out on something big?
7 If you had an unlimited supply of money for one week, what would be the top three items on your shopping list?

CD-ROM   For more activities go to **Things Unit 3**

4 I could kick myself

LEARNING AIMS

- Can talk about hypothetical situations in the past
- Can use the language of advertising
- Can write a letter of complaint

Lead-in

1 Work in groups. Write a popular product name for each of these items: a car, a soft drink, a perfume, a chocolate bar, a sportswear label.

Example: car – *VW Golf*, soft drink – *Diet Coke*, perfume – *Opium*

2 Which of the product names do you like best? Which do you think suits the product best? Give reasons for your answers.

3 Do you think it is easy to come up with names for new products? What do you think the problems could be?

Reading and vocabulary

1 🔘 **24** Read the article on page 47. How many companies faced problems associated with naming a product?

2 Read the text again. Match these summaries to the paragraphs. Look for key words to help you.

a	Many mistakes are made when choosing a name for the world market.	3
b	Cosmetic companies pay the price for their ignorance.	4
c	Getting it wrong could prove embarrassing or funny.	1
d	Soft drink and fast food companies make unappetising promises.	6
e	Vegetables fail to sell as buyers are scared away.	2
f	Do your homework right and you could end up with a bestselling product.	8
g	It's not what it means – it's how you pronounce it.	5
h	Made *of* babies or *for* them?	7

3 Find words and phrases in the text which mean:

1 starting to sell a new product to the public (paragraph 2) launching
2 a planned set of publicity material (paragraph 2) ad campaign
3 a company that makes a product (paragraph 3) manufacturer
4 world sales area (paragraph 3) global market
5 a short, memorable phrase used to advertise something (paragraph 6) slogan
6 people who buy and use a product (paragraph 7) consumer
7 something that is very well known (paragraph 8) household name
8 products that have their own name made by a particular company (paragraph 8) brand

4 Complete these sentences with words in Ex 3. Make any necessary changes.

Example: Coca-Cola is the world's most popular *brand* of soft drink.

1 McDonald's is so famous it has become a household name.
2 General Motors is the world's biggest car manufacturer.
3 According to a survey, Nike's *Just do it* is the most recognised advertising slogan in the world.
4 Microsoft has dominated the global software market since the mid-1980s.
5 European consumers buy half of the world's chocolate.
6 The world's longest-running ad campaign is for Andrex toilet tissue. It was launched in the UK in 1972 and is still going strong.

'What's in a name? Just ask the man behind the launching of a thousand new identities' by Alistair Miller for *The Times*

What's in a name?

1   Coming up with catchy product names is a lot harder than you may imagine, especially in this Global Age, when a word that might inspire admiration in one country can just as easily inspire red faces or unintended amusement in another.

2   For instance, if an American company had consulted linguists before launching their 'Jolly Green Giant' vegetables in the Arab world, their advertising campaign may have been more successful, as they would have discovered that it translates as 'Intimidating Green Ogre*'.

3   This is just one in a catalogue of expensive and damaging errors made by manufacturers on the global market, where brand-naming is a minefield* of linguistic complexity.

4   Even the biggest manufacturers make costly mistakes. If two multinational cosmetic manufacturers had known that 'mist' is German for 'manure*', they could have saved themselves a great deal of money. But in the event, Clairol had to take their 'Mist Stick' hair curler off the market and Estée Lauder had to rename their 'Country Mist' hairspray.

5   Toyota fell into a similar trap with its MR2 in France. This time it wasn't a question of meaning, but pronunciation. If only they had tried saying 'MR2' out loud in French, they would have realised that it sounds like the sort of thing a dog would leave on a pavement.

6   Slogans don't always translate well either. Pepsi's late-60s slogan 'Come alive with the Pepsi generation' was loosely translated into Mandarin Chinese as 'Pepsi will bring back your ancestors from the dead'. And KFC must wish they had been paying more attention when the slogan 'finger-lickin' good' was mistranslated in China as 'eat your fingers off'. Not the most appetizing image.

7   Cultural problems are not always of a linguistic nature. Manufacturers should have been aware that in parts of Africa, consumers are used to seeing a picture on the label of what's inside the container. With this in mind, it's not difficult to imagine why 'Oopsie Boo-Boo' baby food, with a picture of a smiling baby on the label, was received on that continent with some suspicion.

8   Thus, inspiration and imagination are not enough when it comes to naming a product. Manufacturers need to ask themselves questions like, 'What does the word mean in Arabic, Polish or any other language used by potential customers? Can it be pronounced?' But get it right and the products could become household names, such as the top three brands in the world: Marlboro, Coca-Cola and Budweiser.

Glossary

*ogre = a large, frightening person in children's stories

*minefield = a situation or process with many possible problems or dangers

*manure = solid waste from farm animals

LANGUAGE STUDY

Unreal past and regrets

if (only), *wish* and *should have*

1   Look at these extracts from the text and answer the questions.

a   *If an American company* **had consulted** *linguists before launching their 'Jolly Green Giant' vegetables in the Arab world, … they* **would have discovered** *that it translates as 'Intimidating Green Ogre'.*

b   *If only they* **had tried** *saying 'MR2' out loud …*

c   *KFC must wish they* **had been paying** *more attention when the slogan 'finger-lickin' good' was mistranslated in China as 'eat your fingers off'.*

d   *Manufacturers* **should have been** *aware that in parts of Africa, consumers are used to seeing a picture on the label of what's inside the container.*

1   Do the verbs in **bold** refer to things that happened or things that didn't happen?

2   Which tense follows *if*, *if only* and *wish*?

3   Sentences a and d contain *would have* and *should have*. Which of these is used to talk about:
a   consequences?
b   the correct or better thing to do?

4   Which verb form follows *would have* and *should have*?

Grammar reference page 59

2   Complete this text with the correct form of the verbs.

When Coca-Cola was first shipped to China, the product was named something that sounded like 'Coca-Cola'. If they (1 do) *had done* their homework, they (2 realise) *would have realised* that it translated as 'Bite the young frog'. If only they (3 spot) *had spotted* the mistake before tens of thousands of signs had been printed.

An American T-shirt maker must wish they (4 never / agree) *had never agreed* to print shirts which promoted the Pope's visit to Spain in 2003. Then they (5 not / make) *would not have made* one of the most embarrassing translation errors in history. The T-shirts, which should (6 say) *have said* 'I saw the Pope' (*el Papa*), actually read 'I saw the potato' (*la papa*).

A recent advertising campaign in Italy for drinks company Schweppes (7 be) *would have been* much more successful if someone (8 not / translate) *had not have translated* 'tonic water' as 'toilet water'.

3   🔘 **25** Listen and check your answers to Ex 2. How are *had*, *would* and *have* pronounced?

4   Have you ever made an embarrassing or humorous translation error, or language mistake?

5   Work with a partner. Think about any regrets you have connected with the topics in the box. Say what you should have done instead and what would have happened if you had done things differently.

Examples: *I wish I'd taken studying English more seriously at school. If I had, I …*

If only I'd spoken to that guy I met at the party last month. I'm sure we would have …

> something you bought   a holiday / travel   your studies   a boyfriend / girlfriend
> someone you met   job / work   family   a party   money

Music and advertising

Listening

1   🔘 **26** Listen to five pieces of music and write down adjectives that you associate with each one. Then compare your ideas with a partner.

2   The pieces of music are extracts from TV adverts for the products illustrated. Listen again and guess which product goes with which piece of music.

3   🔘 **27** Listen to the creative team of an advertising agency discussing the products and the music they have chosen for each commercial. Check your answers to Ex 2.

4   Listen again and complete these sentences.

    1   Soul music from the sixties _____ old black and white movies.

    2   This is the kind of music _____ family holidays when I was a kid.

    3   When I _____ and _____ to this, I _____ Verona.

    4   Hip hop _____ cool.

    5   This track _____ the most romantic evening I've ever had.

5   Work with a partner. Use the words and phrases in Ex 4 to talk about the music you associate with different occasions or times in your life.

    Example: *Hip hop takes me back to when I lived in New York.*

6   Work in groups. Decide which music you would like to have with you on a desert island.

Writing

1   Read the letter of complaint to an internet service provider and answer these questions.

    1   What did the customer order? What does he want to happen next?

    2   How does the writer show that he's dissatisfied? What tone does he use?

2   The letter contains a mixture of formal and informal language. Underline the parts of the letter that are appropriate in a formal letter of complaint.

3   Write a letter of complaint based on the model in Ex 2. Decide on the product and what was wrong with it. Use these key expressions.

    writing / complain about / placed an order with you for / since then / encountered numerous problems / specific details / as follows / now writing to inform / intend to cancel my order / must insist / full refund / close my account with immediate effect / otherwise / no alternative / seek legal action

---

Dear Sir or Madam

I am writing to complain about the appalling service provided by your company. Three months ago I saw your advert, and in a moment of madness, I placed an order with you for installation of a cable modem. Since then, I have encountered numerous problems, as well as ignorance and stupidity of unimaginable proportions.

The specific details are as follows. My initial installation was cancelled without warning. I then wasted an entire Saturday twiddling my thumbs waiting for your technician. When he did not arrive, I spent a further 57 minutes hanging onto your no-helpline listening to a robot telling me to look at your website. HOW???

The rescheduled installation then took place two weeks later, although the technician forgot to bring the modem, as well as his brain. Two weeks later, the technician had still not returned. After 15 telephone calls over a four-week period, the modem was finally installed. Better late than never I thought. However, the modem stopped working two days later and it has not worked since.

As I am sick and tired of talking to a robot, I am now writing to inform you that I intend to cancel my order with you. You have probably given up reading this by now, as no doubt you have a thousand other dissatisfied customers to ignore; but for the record, I must insist that you send me a full refund and close my account with immediate effect. Otherwise, I will have no alternative but to seek legal advice.

Yours faithfully

CD-ROM   For more activities go to **Things Unit 4**

5 Review

Lead-in 1 Work with a partner. Which of these statements do you think apply to men and which to women? They:

1 enjoy shopping even if they don't buy anything.
2 only go shopping if they need something.
3 don't like to return things to a shop because it suggests they made a mistake.
4 feel that the name on the shopping bag is as important as what's in it.
5 enjoy hunting for a bargain.

Shop 'til you drop

1 Complete the article with the words and phrases in the box.

brand	saved	their best	good impression	snapping up	splashed out

2 Read the text again and compare your ideas in Lead-in Ex 1 with the author's.

HOW TO SHOP

Shops are the only places in society where people ask you if you need help. They'll do (1) _____ to treat you like the attractive and interesting person you could become if you (2) _____ on the most expensive items in the shop.

Shopping is not the same as buying; women shop, men buy. Women can enjoy shopping without buying something. They can even go shopping, take stuff back and still have fun. Men go to the shops only when they need something. They look for this thing, and when they find it, they buy it. If it's not right, they don't take it back because this would imply some error of judgement on their part.

For women, the golden rule of shopping is that the more trendy and exclusive the (3) _____ name on the bag, the better you will feel. And a bag with little ropes instead of handles is almost worth buying on its own. Once you have about five bags, put some of the bags into the other bags. Remember, if you want to make a (4) _____, rather than putting small into big, you should put cheap into expensive.

On the other hand, bargains can also be an exciting part of shopping. Women enjoy (5) _____ a bargain, and they will often finish a shopping trip claiming to have (6) _____ more money than they've spent.

Men and women should never shop together. If they do, the correct position for the man is just outside the door of the shop. The woman then summons the man to look at something she has no intention of buying. This is repeated in every shop, except the one with interesting gadgets for men.

3 Work with a partner. Do you agree with the author's ideas? Which of the things he mentions have you done or experienced?

4 Imagine you are conducting a survey about shopping habits. Rewrite the direct questions as indirect questions using the question beginnings in the box. Add one or two questions of your own.

Could you tell me	Would you say	Do you mind if I ask you	Do you know

1 How often do you go shopping?
2 Is shopping generally a pleasure or a necessity for you?
3 Do you generally go shopping alone or with friends?
4 How much do you spend on clothing each month?
5 Do you ever buy clothes without trying them on?
6 How often do you take clothes back to the shop?
7 When are you next going shopping?

5   Ask your classmates (males and females) the questions in Ex 4 and record their answers. In your class, is there a difference in the way the sexes shop?

6   Do you think men or women are bigger consumers of gadgets and electronic items? Why?

7   Complete the text with an appropriate form of the verbs. Use the present simple, present continuous or present perfect.

The sound of beeping behind a closed bedroom door used to mean one thing: a teenager, or his dad, playing with the latest hi-tech boys' toy. Nowadays, however, inventors (1 begin) _____ to realise that the fastest growing market is girls' gadgets.

Women (2 spend) _____ more than ever before on cameras, laptops and mobile phones. Other gadgets popular with women are the pedometer, a device which (3 count) _____ the number of steps a person (4 take) _____, and digital music players.

The high street chain 'the Gadget Shop' now (5 have) _____ a 50:50 split of male and female customers. Its founder, Jonathan Elvidge, said, 'I (6 think) _____ technology (7 always / appeal) _____ to women but it hasn't been targeted the right way before.'

A recent survey found that women (8 spend) _____ nearly 300 euros a year on new technology, just 50 euros less than men. GirlsStuff.co.uk, the online retailer, (9 record) _____ an 800% increase in the last four months. But the most surprising statistic is one revealed by a recent survey conducted by the Consumer Electronics Association: women (10 change) _____ their minds about their ideal gift. Forget the old saying 'diamonds are a girl's best friend'. Today, a majority of women would prefer a state-of-the-art TV to a one-carat diamond ring.

8   What are your favourite gadgets and electronic items? What was the last gadget you bought? If you could have any gadget, what would it be? Discuss your answers with a partner.

If only I'd checked

1   🔘 **28** Listen to three people talking about something they regretted. Match the names of the people to the pictures. Who were the presents for and why?

Dan ☐   Becky ☐   Greg ☐

2   🔘 **29** What do you think went wrong? Listen to the second part of their stories to find out.

3   Complete these extracts with the correct form of the verbs.

1   I should (ask) _____ her what she wanted, then I wouldn't (make) _____ that mistake.

2   If only I (check) _____ what it meant.

3   But if I (tell) _____ her, it would (spoil) _____ the surprise.

4   I wish I (never / have) _____ the stupid idea in the first place.

4   Work with a partner. Think about a time when you bought either a present for someone or something for yourself and then regretted it. Tell your partner about it. Use *I wish … / If (only) … / I should / shouldn't have …*

Song

1   Read the factfile about Yvonne Fair and answer these questions.

    1   What is the significance of the dates 1942, 1976 and 1994?

    2   What connects Yvonne Fair with the soul legends James Brown, Gladys Knight and Dionne Warwick?

    3   What connects Yvonne Fair with pop star Robbie Williams?

    4   In what way was her career disappointing?

factfile

Born in Las Vegas in 1942, Yvonne Fair started singing professionally in the early 1960s. She signed with the Motown record label and toured for five years as a member of James Brown's backing group. But it was her version of Gladys Knight's *It should have been me* that brought her most attention when it became an international hit in 1976. Yvonne Fair's amazingly powerful voice should have made her a big star of rhythm and blues, but she never capitalised on the success of *It should have been me*. She appeared in a minor role as a singer in the film *Lady sings the blues*, and before her untimely death in Las Vegas in 1994 she worked with Dionne Warwick. Recently, Yvonne Fair's version of *It should have been me* was chosen to be on the CD *Bridget Jones's diary 2* alongside other classics by artists such as Van Morrison, Robbie Williams and Diana Ross.

2   🔘 **30** Listen to the song and answer these questions.

    1   Where is the singer?   2   How is she feeling?   3   Why?

It should have been me

I saw my love walking down the aisle
As he passed me by, he turned to me and gave me a smile
Then the preacher, then the preacher, the preacher joined their hands
All the people, the people began to stand
When I shouted,

'It should have been me. It should have been me
You know, it should have been me
Baby, how can you do this to me?'

You made a promise that we'd never part
Then you turned around and you broke my heart
Now you're standing there saying 'I do'
Holding hands with somebody new

When you know that it should have been me
It should have been me. It should have been me
Baby, how can you do this to me?

Then the preacher, the preacher asked that there be silence, please
'If any objections to this wedding,
Speak now or forever, forever hold your peace.'
And I stood up and said,

'It should have been me. It should have been me'
Jumped out of my seat and screamed
'It should have been me
You're blowing my mind
People believe me that man is mine
It should have been me. It should have been me. It should have been me
Somebody call the police
That woman down there is a doggone thief'

3 Put the summary of the song in the correct order.

a   up if they had any objections to the marriage, I stood up and said, 'You're making ☐

b   a promise to stay with me forever. If he had kept his promise, it would ☐

c   As I watched the man I love getting married to someone else, it took ☐1

d   my best to stay calm, but when the preacher asked for people to speak ☐

e   how much this is hurting me? You've broken my heart.' ☐

f   me back to the time when he was with me. At that time, he had made ☐

g   have been me walking down the aisle with him. During the ceremony, I did ☐

h   a big mistake! You're with the wrong person. Have you any idea ☐

4 Have you ever been in a situation where you thought 'It should have been me.'? Discuss your ideas with a partner.

Guess our words

1 Read how to play 'Guess our words' and play the game.

How to play

1   The game is played in two teams, A and B.

2   The teams write down five words for each of their categories – making sure that the other team does not overhear!

3   The teams sit facing each other. Team A reads out the title of their first category and Team B has one minute to say as many words as possible under that category. If they say a word that Team A has on their piece of paper, Team B gets 1 point. Team A is responsible for marking down the points and timing Team B.

4   Now it's Team B's turn to read out the title of their first category and Team A has one minute to say Team B's words.

5   The teams continue taking turns to guess the words for all the categories.

Team A

Write down …

- 5 adjectives that describe the taste of food
- 5 nouns that collocate with make
- 5 gadgets used by men and women
- 3 'money' verbs that contain the sound /eɪ/
- 3 phrasal verbs connected with using the phone
- 2 ways of saying you're short of money

Team B

Write down …

- 5 adjectives that describe the texture of food
- 5 nouns that collocate with do
- 5 words from the world of advertising
- 3 'money' verbs that contain the sound /e/
- 3 phrasal verbs connected with new products and shopping
- 2 ways of talking about memories and associations

Extra practice

Unit 1

1 Put the words in the box into the correct group.

> spicy   crisp   salty   juicy   tough   sweet
> chewy   soggy   buttery   tangy   crusty
> creamy   sickly   greasy   sour   bland
> crunchy   mild   tender   gooey

Positive / Neutral: _____

_____

_____

Negative: _____

_____

2 Cross out the word which is **not** possible.
1 The soup we had was OK, but a bit
   salty | bland | soggy.
2 The salad was lovely – very *crisp | crunchy | crusty.*
3 My curry wasn't bad, but a bit too
   hot | spicy | juicy for me.
4 The vegetables were really *tender | crusty | crisp.*
5 The chocolate pudding was very *mild | sickly | gooey.*
6 The fruits were really *tangy | spicy | juicy.*
7 We finished off with some wonderful
   gooey | creamy | crisp French cheese.

3 These questions are from an interview with celebrity chef Jamie Oliver. Rewrite them as indirect questions.
1 What was your first job?
   Could you tell me _____ ?
2 Did you always want to be a chef?
   And would you say _____ ?

3 How did you become involved with television?
    I'm interested to know_____ ?
4 Why are your cookbooks so popular with men?
    Why do you think _____ ?
5 What is your favourite meal?
    Could you tell me _____ ?
6 Is there anything you absolutely won't eat?
    I was wondering _____ ?
7 What would you recommend for a simple, but romantic dish to impress someone?
    I'd like to know_____ ?

4 Match the questions in Ex 3 to these answers.
a My mum's Sunday dinner with all those vegetables from the garden. Best roast potatoes in the world.
b I grew up in a little pub restaurant. It belonged to my parents. I started cooking with my dad when I was about eight for pocket money.
c Chicken feet. You have to be very, very over-hungry if you want to eat chicken feet, because they're horrible.
d There was a one-off documentary for the BBC. I was busy working hard and the camera came over. I was just having a laugh, really, telling them what I was doing. They loved it.
e Not really. I just found it the easiest thing, at a young age, to do to make money.
f Anything can be romantic. It's nice to have things in the middle of the table, things you can share.
g I don't know. It's probably because they're useless and their girlfriends are saying 'get this young guy's books'.

5 Think of a celebrity that you are interested in. Complete the questions to ask him / her.

Celebrity's name: _____

1 Could you tell me _____
   _____ ?
2 I'd like to know _____
   _____ ?
3 I was wondering _____
   _____ ?
4 Do you think _____
   _____ ?
5 Have you any idea _____
   _____ ?
6 Would you say _____
   _____ ?
7 Do you mind if I ask you _____
   _____ ?

Unit 2

1 Complete this newspaper article with the phrasal verbs in the box.

| brought out   get off   come up with |
| run into   keep up with   set off |

A phoney excuse

Anyone late for work or somewhere they shouldn't be can now use mobile phones to cover their tracks. IT company Simeda has (1) _____ the idea of an 'audible alibi' to convince someone that you really are somewhere else. The phone will play background sounds such as 'road works' or 'at the dentist' to add electronic weight to an excuse. If you oversleep and want your boss to think you have already (2) _____ for work and have (3) _____ heavy traffic, the 'traffic jam' soundtrack will supply engine noise from your bedroom. The system also features a ringing telephone, as if you are receiving another call, to provide an excuse to (4) _____ the phone. So far, the company has (5) _____ nine different backing tracks but Simeda has yet to (6) _____ picture phone technology and devise false visual backgrounds.

2 Replace the underlined words with the correct form of the phrasal verbs in the box. You may need to change the word order.

| come down   bring out   call back |
| come out   get off   get through to |
| run out of   pick up   top up   snap up |

1 When MP3s <u>were first introduced</u>, people <u>quickly bought</u> them.

2 DVDs have <u>been reduced</u> in price a lot since they <u>first sold</u> them.

3 I can't <u>make contact with</u> Giselle. I don't seem to be able to <u>receive</u> a signal for my phone.

4 I need to <u>buy more credit for</u> my phone – I'm just about to <u>use all the</u> credit.

5 I'll <u>call</u> you <u>again</u> later. I've got to <u>stop using</u> the phone – my friend needs to make a call.

3 Find eight gadgets in the word snake.

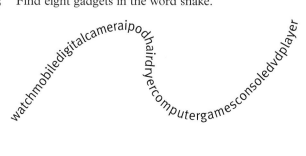

4 Complete Sara's email to her friend with the correct form of *make* or *do*.

New Message

To: samp@hotmail.com
Cc:
Subject: Just to say hi

Hi Sam
Just a quick email to say hi and to let you know I'm having a great time here. I'm (1) _____ an English course here in Brighton and I've (2) _____ lots of new friends. The lessons are fun, but we get loads of work to (3) _____ – a bit too much if you ask me. Anyway, I'm learning a lot and I've decided to (4) _____ the IELTS exam again! I think I need to (5) _____ a bit more effort than before – hopefully I won't (6) _____ such a mess of it this time! Outside school I'm trying to (7) _____ quite a lot in the evenings, like going to pubs and clubs. Next weekend, a few of us are going to London for the day.
By the way, could you (8) _____ me a favour? Can you send me Frank and Ginka's email addresses? Thanks.
Must go now but I'll drop you another line soon.

Love
Sara x

5 Write a brief email to a friend telling them your news. Use some of the *make* and *do* expressions in Ex 4.

6 Complete these responses with the words in the box.

| kidding   off   surprise   way   wrong |

1 **A:** I just heard that they're hoping to put someone on Mars in the next 10 years.
  B: No (1) _____! Are you sure?

2 **A:** Do you happen to know when email was invented?
  B: Well, I might be (2) _____, but I'd say it was in the early 1970s.

3 **A:** I read the other day that we'll all have computer chips in our heads in the next twenty years.
  B: You're (3) _____! In the next 20 years?

4 **A:** I heard that Bill Gates – you know, the boss of Microsoft – earns a million dollars a day!
  B: Come (4) _____ it! A million a day!

5 **A:** I read in the paper that London is the city with the most billionaires in the world?
  B: It wouldn't (5) _____ me.

Unit 3

1 Complete the crossword with the missing money verbs from the clues.

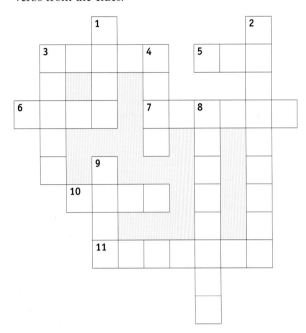

Across

3 In the biggest single robbery ever thieves _____ gems worth $100 million.

5 The biggest lottery prize to date which was _____ by a single person is $315 million.

6 When he died in 2001, American publisher Walter Annenberg _____ his $1 billion art collection to the Metropolitan Museum of Art in New York City.

7 The London Marathon _____ more money for charity than any other sporting event.

10 In 1992, businessman George Soros gambled $10 billion that the British pound would fall in value. He was right and overnight he _____ $1 billion.

11 In August 1999, Bill and Melinda Gates _____ $6 billion to the charitable foundation they had set up.

Down

1 In 2002, internet company AOL _____ $98.7 billion – at the time, the biggest loss in US history.

2 When she _____ $5 billion at the age of 18, Athina Onassis Roussel became the richest teenager in the world.

3 Holidaymakers from the US _____ over $60 billion a year. Germany and the UK are the next biggest spenders.

4 Thirty years after his death, the Elvis Presley estate continues to _____ about $40 million a year.

8 Warren Buffett, the world's richest investor, took his first step into high finance when he _____ $100 in a local company at the age of eleven.

9 In 1999, American Marc Ostrofsky sold the domain name 'business.com' for $7.5 million. He had _____ only $150,000 for it two years earlier.

2 Match the sentence beginning to the endings.
1 Studying has never been my
2 I'd say I've got quite a competitive
3 My bank account is in the
4 I'm constantly setting myself new
5 I think I've got quite a lot of business
6 I've got a bit of money put aside for a rainy
7 Nothing in life has been handed to me on a

a red.   b forte.   c acumen.   d streak.
e plate.   f goals.   g day.

3 Tick the statements in Ex 2 which describe you.

4 Match these pairs of questions to the correct answers.

1 What do you do?   Preparing a lesson.
   What are you doing?   I'm a teacher.

2 Have you seen Steve?   Not much these days.
   Do you see Steve?   Yes, this morning actually.

3 Are you staying here long? Two weeks so far.
   Have you been here long?   Just one more week.

4 How do you feel about it? In my opinion, it's great.
   How are you feeling?   I'm better than yesterday.

5 Read about the symbolism of the US one-dollar bill. Complete the text with the correct present or present perfect form of the verbs.

According to the US treasury, billions of one-dollar bills (1 currently / circulate) _____ worldwide. They (2 account for) _____ about 45% of all the notes printed. But how many of us know what the images on the bill actually are? On the front of the note is a portrait of the first president, George Washington. He (3 appear) _____ on the bill since 1869.

On the reverse, the Great Seal of the United States (4 show) _____ an American eagle behind the national shield. The eagle (5 hold) _____ a 13-leaved olive branch in one of its claws and 13 arrows in the other. These images (6 symbolise) _____ the struggle between peace and war. The 13-letter motto 'E Pluribus Unum' means 'out of many, one' and (7 refer) _____ to the formation of the United States from the 13 original colonies in 1776.

On the left, there is an unfinished pyramid which (8 signify) _____ that the United States will always grow and improve. At the foot of the pyramid are the Roman numerals for 1776. The pyramid has 13 steps and is topped by the all-seeing eye, which (9 constantly / look) _____ to the future.

The one-dollar bill (10 have) _____ the same design since 1955.

Unit 4

1 Complete the article with the words in the box.

> brand   advertising campaign
> household name   consumers   launch
> manufacturer   product   market

Coca-Cola fails to tap into European water market

Dasani, the second-biggest-selling
(1) _____ of bottled water in
America, was by now supposed to be on
everybody's lips. Its parent company,
Coca-Cola, the world's biggest soft-drinks
(2) _____, had lined up a £10-
million (3) _____ in an attempt to
make Dasani a (4) _____ in Europe.
Its centrepiece was to be a £1-million, 30-second
television ad showing Dasani flowing through a
city's streets, but the (5) _____ was
cancelled.

So, what went wrong? Perhaps Coca-Cola didn't
do enough research on the lucrative European
(6) _____ . With safe tap water the
norm in most of Europe, bottled water is a
'luxury' item, which is advertised with an
emphasis on its source and its character as much
as on its purity. In other words, European
(7) _____ are buying more than just
H_2O.

Dasani bottled water came from the taps of a
factory just outside London. When the news
leaked out that Dasani was no more than city tap
water with a few minerals added, it earned
Coca-Cola so much bad publicity that a few
weeks later the (8) _____ was
taken off the shelves altogether.

2 Write two sentences for each person beginning with
I wish I had(n't) …, *If I / you had(n't) …* and *I /You
should(n't) have …* .

1 _____

_____

2 _____

_____

3 _____

_____

3 Complete this newspaper story with the correct form
of the verbs.

Hotel boss in hot water

Hotel guest, Sally Burchell must wish she
(1 never / decide) _____ to
write her letter of complaint to the manager of
the Atlantic Hotel in Newquay, UK. In reply,
the managing director, Anthony Cobley, wrote a
scathing letter to Ms Burchell, who had
complained about being refused a glass of tap
water with her meal.

In the letter, he told Ms Burchell he felt 'the
need to enlighten you to the workings of the
modern world. If only you (2 stop) _____
_____ to think, you (3 realise) _____
_____ immediately why you were
refused the tap water.' He continued, 'I buy the
ice and lemon that goes into the water and the
labour to cut the lemon and serve the water. I
provide the luxury surroundings for the water to
be drunk in and I pay for the glass to be washed
after you've used it. And you think that I should
(4 provide) _____ all of this to
you free of charge.'

'I just find it appalling that a hotel or any
other sort of business would talk to its customers
like this. I just wish I (5 not / go) _____
_____ there in the first place,' Ms Burchell
said. 'I spent over £40 on my meal and they
should (6 give) _____ me the
water without question. If they (7 do) _____
_____ so, then this ridiculous fuss
(8 be / avoided) _____.'

4 Think of a time when you received bad service in a
shop / restaurant. If this has never happened to you,
invent a situation. Write a short letter of complaint
to the manager. Refer to the letter of complaint on
page 49.

5 Put the words in brackets in the correct order to
complete the sentences.

1 Eating olives (makes / always / me / of / think)
_____ Greece – I was on
holiday there as a child when I first ate one.

2 Whenever I smell incense, (of / I / think /
immediately) _____ India.
You can smell it everywhere over there.

3 Listening to U2 (back / to / takes / when / me)
_____ I was in my early
teens. I never stopped playing their stuff.

4 The song *Beautiful* by Christina Aguilera
(remind / of / will / always / me)
_____ my first girlfriend.

Grammar reference

Unit 1

Indirect questions

Form

Indirect questions begin with a question phrase:

Could you tell me …?
I'd like to know …?
I just wanted to know …?
Do you know …?
Do you happen to know …?
Have you any idea …?
I was wondering …?
Do you mind if I ask you …?
Would you say …?

The question phrase is followed by a question word or *if*:
*Could you tell me **how much** fresh fruit and vegetables you eat?*

*I was wondering **if** you'd like to come with us?*

The word order changes from the direct question form and the subject comes before the verb. You do not use the auxiliary verb *do*:
*Do you know how old **he is**?* NOT *Do you know how old is he?*

*Have you any idea where **she went**?* NOT *Have you any idea where **did she go**?*

You can sometimes use the past tense to help create greater 'distance' between speaker and listener. This is most common after question phrases that contain a past tense:
*I **was** wondering if there **was** anything I **could** eat that **would** boost my memory?*

*I just **wanted** to know if you **were** still coming with us tonight?*

Use

You use indirect questions when you want to be more tentative, for example when the question is sensitive or personal, or when you don't want to put pressure on the person being asked. You also use indirect questions when you want to sound more formal or polite.

Unit 2

Types of phrasal verbs

A phrasal verb consists of verb + particle(s). The particle is either an adverb or preposition. In three-part verbs, there are two particles.

When you see or hear a phrasal verb, it's important to know which type it is, whether it takes an object and in which position you can put the object. Look carefully at how phrasal verbs are used in context and check in a dictionary.

In *Move* upper-intermediate, we have focused on four basic types of phrasal verb:

Type 1

Type 1 verbs do <u>not</u> have an object. They are also known as 'intransitive phrasal verbs'.
*We **set off** at 7.30.*
*Prices have **come down** again.*

Types 2, 3 and 4

Types 2, 3 and 4 <u>must</u> have an object. They are also known as 'transitive phrasal verbs'.

Type 2

If the object is a noun, it can usually go between the verb and the particle <u>or</u> after the particle:
*They're **bringing a new model out** next month.*
*They're **bringing out a new model** next month.*

If the object is a pronoun, it must go <u>between</u> the verb and the particle:
*They're **bringing it out** next month.*
NOT *They're bringing out it next month.*

There are a few type 2 phrasal verbs where the object cannot go after the particle. This is a matter of usage and there are no general rules:
I'll call Sam back. NOT *I'll call back Sam.*

It's difficult to tell the cameras apart. NOT *It's difficult to tell apart the cameras.*

Type 3

The object must go <u>after</u> the particle:
*I **ran into** Belinda last week.*
*I've been **looking for it** for ages.*

Type 4

These phrasal verbs have two particles. The object must go <u>after</u> the second particle:
*They can't **keep up with** demand.*
*I've always **looked up to** her.*

Unit 3

Talking about the present

Present simple

You use the present simple to talk about:
– facts and things that are seen as true in general:
Everyone's good at something.
*I **live** in Paris.*
*Several countries now **have** the euro.*

– things that happen all the time or happen repeatedly:
*I **get** to meet so many different kinds of people.*
*He **travels** a lot for his job.*
*I usually **get up** at 7.30.*

– states (even when we consider them to be temporary):
*I **don't have** a flashy car.*
*He **seems** nice.*
*I **don't understand**.*
*It **tastes** great.*

Here are some common 'state' verbs (verbs that don't usually have a continuous form):

Feelings: want, like, love, admire, prefer, hate, surprise

Thoughts: believe, know, feel, realise, think, understand, suppose, imagine

Possession: belong, have (got), possess, own, consist

Spatial relationship: fit, include, involve, lack, reach, contain

Senses: feel, hear, see, smell, sound, taste

Appearance: appear, look like, seem

Present continuous

You use the present continuous to talk about:
– something temporary that is in progress at the moment of speaking:

*I'm **having** my own house built at the moment.*
*I'm **reading** a fantastic book.*
*He's **doing** his homework right now.*

– changing situations / trends:
*My English **is getting** better day by day.*
*More and more people **are becoming** millionaires.*

Present perfect

You use the present perfect to connect a present situation with something that happened or started in the past:

– when something that happened in the past has an important consequence in the present:
*Everything I have, I've **earned** myself.*
*I've **lost** my mobile.* (I can't use it now)
*Have you ever **been** to New York?* (I want to ask you about it)

– when something started in the past and continues to the present. You use *for* and *since* and expressions such as *all my life* and *always* to indicate the duration or starting point:
*All my life, I've **been** around cars.*
*She's **worked** here since 2003.*
*We've **been waiting** for over half an hour.*

will

You can use *will* to express a habit that is typical or predictable:

*When I get to work, I'll **drive** whatever car happens to be on the forecourt.*
*Most weekends, I'll **go out** for a few drinks with some friends.*

Note: this is not a substitute for the use of present simple for habits.

Unit 4

Unreal past and regrets

If ...
Form

If	past perfect	*would have* + past participle

You can sometimes use other modal verbs such as *might, may, could,* instead of *would* etc:

*If they'd done more research, their advertising campaign **might have been** more successful.*

*I'm sure I **could have passed** the exam, if I'd worked harder.*

If + past perfect + *would have* + past participle is sometimes known as the 'third conditional'.

Use

You use *If* + past perfect + *would have* + past participle to talk about unreal situations and their hypothetical consequences in the past:
*If I'd **known** about the job, I would have applied for it.* (I didn't know about the job)

*If the lessons had been a bit more interesting, I'd have **learned** a lot more.* (I didn't learn a lot more)

If only /wish

Form

If only /wish	past perfect

Use

You use *If only / wish* + past perfect to express regret about something that happened or didn't happen in the past:
*If only I'd **realised** he'd be so upset.* (I didn't realise)
*I really **wish** I hadn't told him.* (I told him)

should have
Form

should have	past participle

Use

You can use *should have* + past participle to talk about what was the correct or better thing to do:
I shouldn't have been so angry with him. (I was angry with him)
What do you think I should have done?

Wordlist

*** the 2,500 most common English words, ** very common words, * fairly common words

Unit 1

asparagus n /ə'spærəgəs/
avocado n /ˌævə'kɑːdəʊ/
avoid v /ə'vɔɪd/ ***
bland adj /blænd/
blow (your) top phrase /ˌbləʊ (jə) 'tɒp/
boost v /buːst/ **
brain food n /'breɪn ˌfuːd/
broccoli n /'brɒkəli/
calcium n /'kælsiəm/ *
chewy adj /'tʃuːi/
comfort food n /'kʌmfət ˌfuːd/
concentration (of something) n
   /ˌkɒnsn'treɪʃn (əv sʌmθɪŋ)/ ***
crisp adj /krɪsp/ *
crunchy adj /'krʌntʃi/ *
deficiency n /dɪ'fɪʃnsi/
Do you mind if I ask you (...?) phrase /də jə
   ˌmaɪnd ɪf aɪ 'ɑːsk juː/
Don't be so nosey! phrase /ˌdəʊnt ˌbi ˌsəʊ
   'nəʊzi/
fiery adj /'faɪri/
food allergy n /'fuːd ˌælədʒi/
force yourself to v /'fɔːs jəˌself tə/
fresh adj /freʃ/ ***
frozen adj /'frəʊzn/ *
get (someone) down v /ˌget (sʌmwʌn) 'daʊn/
get rid of v /get 'rɪd əv/
ginger biscuit n /ˌdʒɪndʒə 'bɪskɪt/
greasy adj /'griːsi/
health-conscious adj /'helθ ˌkɒnʃəs/
helping n /'helpɪŋ/ *
hot adj /hɒt/ ***
I just wanted to know (where ...) phrase /aɪ
   'dʒʌst ˌwɒntɪd tə ˌnəʊ/
I was wondering (if ...) phrase /aɪ wəz
   'wʌndərɪŋ/
I'd rather not answer that phrase /aɪd ˌrɑːðə
   ˌnɒt 'ɑːnsə ˌðæt/
increase v /ɪn'kriːs/ ***
intake n /'ɪnteɪk/ *
iron n /'aɪən/ **
juicy adj /'dʒuːsi/
keep the best till last phrase /ˌkiːp ðə ˌbest
   tɪl 'lɑːst/
lemon tart n /ˌlemən 'tɑːt/
mild adj /maɪld/ **
moody adj /'muːdi/
nutritious adj /nju:'trɪʃəs/
passion fruit n /'pæʃn ˌfruːt/
pie n /paɪ/ *
proportion n /prə'pɔːʃn/ ***
push (something) round the plate phrase
   /ˌpʊʃ (sʌmθɪŋ) ˌraʊnd ðə 'pleɪt/
rice pudding n /ˌraɪs 'pʊdɪŋ/
salty adj /'sɔːlti/
savoury adj /'seɪvəri/
shortbread biscuit n /ˈʃɔːtbred ˌbɪskɪt/
sickly adj /'sɪkli/
snack n /snæk/ *
snore v /snɔː/
soggy adj /'sɒgi/
sour adj /'saʊə/ *
specialist n /'speʃəlɪst/ **
spicy adj /'spaɪsi/
spot n /spɒt/ ***
sushi n /'suːʃi/
temper n /'tempə/ **
tender adj /'tendə/ **
tough adj /tʌf/ ***
vitamin n /'vɪtəmɪn/ **
Would you say ...? phrase /wʊd jə ˌseɪ/

Unit 2

actually adv /'æktʃuəli/ ***
apparently adv /ə'pærəntli/ ***
basically adv /'beɪsɪkli/ **
battery n /'bætəri/ **
break down v /ˌbreɪk 'daʊn/
bring out v /ˌbrɪŋ 'aʊt/
call back v /ˌkɔːl 'bæk/
call off v /ˌkɔːl 'ɒf/
can't live without phrase /ˌkɑːnt 'lɪv wɪðˌaʊt/
cloning n /'kləʊnɪŋ/
come down v /ˌkʌm 'daʊn/
Come off it! phrase /ˌkʌm 'ɒf ɪt/
come out v /ˌkʌm 'aʊt/

come with v /'kʌm ˌwɪð/
come up with v /ˌkʌm 'ʌp wɪð/
complaint n /kəm'pleɪnt/
computer games console n /kəm'pjuːtə
   ˌgeɪmz ˌkɒnsəʊl/
connection n /kə'nekʃn/ ***
cut off v /ˌkʌt 'ɒf/
deal n /diːl/ *
digital camera n /ˌdɪdʒɪtl 'kæm(ə)rə/
do (someone) a favour phrase /du:
   (sʌmwʌn) ə 'feɪvə/
do (your) best phrase /du: (jə) 'best/
DVD player n /di: vi: 'di: ˌpleɪə/
fill in v /ˌfɪl 'ɪn/
fuss n fʌs/
get hold of v /ˌget 'həʊld əv/
get off v /ˌget 'ɒf/
get through to v /ˌget 'θruː tə/
give up v /ˌgɪv 'ʌp/
hairdryer n /'heəˌdraɪə/
hand in v /ˌhænd 'ɪn/
hang up v /ˌhæŋ 'ʌp/
I might be wrong phrase /aɪ ˌmaɪt bi 'rɒŋ/
iPod n /'aɪˌpɒd/
it wouldn't surprise me phrase /ɪt ˌwʊdnt
   sə'praɪz mi/
keep up with v /ˌkiːp 'ʌp wɪð/
look for v /'lʊk fə/
look through v /ˌlʊk 'θruː/
look up v /ˌlʊk 'ʌp/
make a good / bad impression phrase
   /ˌmeɪk ə ˌgʊd, bæd ɪm'preʃn/
make a lot of effort phrase /ˌmeɪk ə ˌlɒt əv
   'efət/
make a mess of (something) phrase /ˌmeɪk ə
   'mes əv (sʌmθɪŋ)/
make an offer phrase /ˌmeɪk ən 'ɒfə/
make money phrase /ˌmeɪk 'mʌni/
mobile n /'məʊbaɪl/ *
No way! phrase /ˌnəʊ 'weɪ/
pick up v /ˌpɪk 'ʌp/
pilotless adj /'paɪlətləs/
print out v /ˌprɪnt 'aʊt/
(low/equal/top) priority phrase /(ˌləʊ,
   ˌiːkwəl, ˌtɒp) praɪ'ɒrəti/
run into v /ˌrʌn 'ɪntuː/
run out of v /ˌrʌn 'aʊt əv/
set off v /ˌset 'ɒf/
snap up v /ˌsnæp 'ʌp/
take off v /ˌteɪk 'ɒf/
texting n /'tekstɪŋ/
throw away v /ˌθrəʊ ə'weɪ/
top up v /ˌtɒp 'ʌp/
try on v /ˌtraɪ 'ɒn/
turn off v /ˌtɜːn 'ɒf/
turn down v /ˌtɜːn 'daʊn/
What do you mean? phrase /ˌwɒt də jə 'miːn/
You're kidding! phrase /jɔː 'kɪdɪŋ/

Unit 3

achieve v /ə'tʃiːv/ ***
be broke phrase /ˌbi 'brəʊk/
be loaded phrase /ˌbi 'ləʊdɪd/
burn v /bɜːn/ **
circulate v /'sɜːkjʊˌleɪt/ **
come into (a sum of) money phrase /ˌkʌm
   ˌɪntə (ə ˌsʌm əv) 'mʌni/
competitive streak n /kəm'petətɪv ˌstriːk/
cost a fortune phrase /ˌkɒst ə 'fɔːtjuːn/
counterfeit money n /ˌkaʊntəfɪt 'mʌni/
donate v /dəʊ'neɪt/ *
earn v /ɜːn/ ***
fake v /feɪk/
find it hard to make ends meet phrase
   /ˌfaɪnd ɪt ˌhɑːd tə ˌmeɪk ˌendz 'miːt/
forte n /'fɔːteɪ/
hand (something) to (someone) on a plate
   phrase /ˌhænd (sʌmθɪŋ) tə (sʌmwʌn) ˌɒn ə
   'pleɪt/
have a weakness for phrase /ˌhæv ə 'wiːknəs
   fɔː/
in the red phrase /ˌɪn ðə 'red/
invest v /ɪn'vest/ ***
leave v /liːv/ ***
lend v /lend/ **
lose v /luːz/ ***
luxuries n /'lʌkʃərɪz/ *

money put by for a rainy day phrase /ˌmʌni
   ˌpʊt ˌbaɪ fə ə ˌreɪni 'deɪ/
natural business acumen n /ˌnætʃ(ə)rəl
   ˌbɪznəs 'ækjʊmən/
official currency n /əˌfɪʃl 'kʌrənsi/
overly ostentatious phrase /ˌəʊvəli
   ˌɒsten'teɪʃəs/
raise v /reɪz/ ***
receive v /rɪ'siːv/ ***
save v /seɪv/ ***
saver n /'seɪvə/
set (one)self clear goals phrase /ˌset
   (wʌn)self ˌklɪə 'gəʊlz/
spend v /spend/ ***
spender n /'spendə/
splash out on v /ˌsplæʃ 'aʊt ɒn/
steal v /stiːl/ ***
the average man in the street phrase /ði
   ˌæv(ə)rɪdʒ ˌmæn ɪn ðə 'striːt/
treat (one)self v /ˌtriːt (wʌn)self/
unlimited adj /ʌn'lɪmɪtɪd/ *
waste v /weɪst/ ***
win v /wɪn/ ***
without the bank balance to match phrase
   /wɪðˌaʊt ðə ˌbæŋk ˌbæləns tə 'mætʃ/

Unit 4

account for v /ə'kaʊnt fɔː/ ***
advertising campaign n /'ædvətaɪzɪŋ
   kæmˌpeɪn/
amusement n /ə'mjuːzmənt/ *
(un)appetising adj /(ʌn)'æpəˌtaɪzɪŋ/
be received phrase /ˌbi rɪ'siːvd/
brand n /brænd/ **
bring back from the dead phrase /ˌbrɪŋ ˌbæk
   frəm ðə 'ded/
catalogue of errors phrase /ˌkætəlɒg əv
   'erəz/
consumer n /kən'sjuːmə/ ***
container n /kən'teɪnə/ **
costly adj /'kɒstli/ *
do (your) homework right phrase /ˌdu: (jə)
   'həʊmwɜːk ˌraɪt/
dominate v /'dɒmɪˌneɪt/ **
global market n /ˌgləʊbl 'mɑːkɪt/
household name n /ˌhaʊshəʊld 'neɪm/
if only phrase /ˌɪf 'əʊnli/
intimidating adj /ɪn'tɪmɪˌdeɪtɪŋ/
launch v /lɔːntʃ/ ***
linguistic complexity n /lɪŋˌgwɪstɪk
   kəm'pleksəti/
make (someone) think of (something)
   phrase /ˌmeɪk (sʌmwʌn) 'θɪŋk əv
   (sʌmθɪŋ)/
manufacturer n /ˌmænjʊ'fæktʃərə/ ***
manure n /mə'njʊə/
meaning n /'miːnɪŋ/ ***
minefield n /'maɪnˌfiːld/
ogre n /'əʊgə/
pronunciation n /prəˌnʌnsi'eɪʃn/
red faces n /ˌred 'feɪsɪz/
remind (someone) of (something) phrase
   /rɪ'maɪnd (sʌmwʌn) əv (sʌmθɪŋ)/
rename v /ˌriː'neɪm/
slogan n /'sləʊgən/ *
sound v /saʊnd/ ***
spot v /spɒt/ **
suspicion n /sə'spɪʃn/ **
take (someone) back to (something) phrase
   /ˌteɪk (sʌmwʌn) ˌbæk tə (sʌmθɪŋ)/
unintended adj /ˌʌnɪn'tendɪd/
visualise v /'vɪzjʊəˌlaɪz/
when I close my eyes and listen phrase
   /ˌwen aɪ ˌkləʊz maɪ ˌaɪz ən (lɪsn/
wish v /wɪʃ/ ***

Communication activities

Unit 1, Reading and speaking Ex 1 page 37

Quiz answers

1b   Healthy-looking snack foods may be lower in sugar but they can often contain more fat. An average cereal bar contains up to 12 grams of fat, whereas a packet of crisps and a small bar of chocolate contain less than 10 grams.

2c   Fizzy drinks are full of sugar. Drink water or fruit juice instead.

3b   This varies from beer to beer, but an average-strength lager contains about 250 calories per bottle.

4c   Ten minutes' walking will burn about 100 calories and is better for all-round aerobic fitness.

5b   Iron carries oxygen around your body. Tiredness, feeling weak and being pale are classic symptoms of iron deficiency.

6c   Broccoli is an excellent source of vitamin C, with 100 grams providing more than three times the daily requirement.

7a   Smoking constricts the blood vessels and prevents nutrients vital to a good complexion from being carried to the skin. It also means that your bloodstream doesn't carry waste products away from your skin. Also, the facial movement and expressions caused by puffing on a cigarette or squinting through smoke will in time cause wrinkles. ('b' and 'c' can also be very bad for the skin if done to excess.)

8a   Fat plays many important roles in the body including keeping us warm, physically protecting our internal organs, providing us with fatty acids which are essential for the functioning of the brain, the heart, blood vessels and many other organs.

9a   Biscuits contain both fat and sugar in large quantities, the perfect combination for weight gain.

10c   Frozen fruit and vegetables can be just as nutritious as fresh vegetables. It's the cooking process which reduces the nutritional value of vegetables.

Student A

Unit 2, Language study Ex 6 page 40

1   Match the phrasal verbs to the nouns.

A   throw away   call off   hang up   turn down   hand in   look up

B   a word   some wastepaper   the music   your coat   the party   your homework

2   Read your sentences to student B and listen to his / her responses. Does he / she give you sensible advice?

    1   Do you think this shirt will fit me?

    2   What shall I do with this form?

    3   I really shouldn't smoke.

    4   I've finished typing the letter – what now?

    5   I'm really hot in this sweater.

    6   There's nothing interesting on TV.

3   Listen to student B's sentences and respond using an appropriate phrasal verb from Ex 1 and the pronoun *it*. All the phrasal verbs are type 2 (must be separated by a pronoun).

    Example:

    A: *What shall I do with this wastepaper?*

    B: *Throw it away.*

Listening scripts

Unit 1 Food for thought

 Listening script 16

Reading text from page 35

 Listening script 17

(FM = Fred Murray, presenter; JW = Joanna Woodward, expert in nutrition; C1 = Caller 1; C2 = Caller 2; C3 = Caller 3)

FM: Welcome to *Fred's phone-in*. I'm Fred Murray and in the studio today I have Joanna Woodward, expert in nutrition. Joanna, congratulations on your latest book *Food for thought* and welcome to *Fred's phone-in*.

JW: Thank you very much. I'm delighted to be here.

FM: Are you ready for our first listener's question?

JW: Absolutely.

FM: Good morning. What's your name and what's your question?

C1: Good morning. My name's Jake and erm, I'm a student. I get pretty good marks most of the time but, well in exams I'm terrible. I know the information, but in an exam situation I forget everything. And I was wondering if there was anything I could eat that would boost my memory?

JW: OK, Jake. First of all, it's quite common for perfectly bright students to fail in exams. I think your problem is one of nerves rather than memory, but the answer to your question is yes, students can boost their memory by watching their diet. You need to increase your intake of so-called brain food like fish. Then make sure you're getting the vitamins you need with as much fresh fruit as you like. All vegetables are good, but the best for you at the moment are broccoli, asparagus and avocados. And here's the secret – two and a half litres of water a day. Did you know that your brain is 85% water?

C1: No, I didn't know that.

JW: OK, so drink plenty of water. Oh, except on the day of the exam of course. Then you need to drink water after the exam, not before!

FM: Yes – good advice. OK, next caller, please.

C2: Hello. My name's Angie and I've got a problem with my skin. I can't get rid of my spots and they're really getting me down. My mum says I eat too much fast food. I just wanted to know if this could be the reason for my skin problem.

JW: Yes, Angie, I'm afraid your mother's probably right. Could you tell me how much fresh fruit and vegetables you eat?

C2: Oh, not much. I eat potatoes – well, chips – but I don't like fruit.

JW: OK, Angie. You need to force yourself to eat five helpings of fruit or vegetables every day – not including chips. If you do this, I can guarantee that your skin will improve.

FM: Right, Joanna, just time for one more before the break. Hello, what's your name and what's your question?

C3: Hi, my name's Jennifer and I'd like to know what I can give my brother for his fiery temper? He's very moody and he blows his top at the smallest thing.

JW: Oh dear, that must be very difficult. Well, you may think that the obvious solution is to keep him away from hot, spicy food. But actually I think your brother might have some sort of food allergy. He needs to visit a specialist for tests.

FM: Jennifer, stay on the line and we'll give you some more information about food allergies. We'll be right back after the break with some more excellent advice on food and nutrition.

Unit 2 State of the art

 Listening script 18

Reading text from page 38

 Listening script 19

(R = Rachel; S = Sheryl; A = Alex)

R: Let's see your new laptop then. Oh it's lovely.

S: It's beautiful, isn't it? I love it.

A: Oh, wow. I bet you sleep with it under your pillow.

S: I do actually.

R: You're kidding!

S: Of course I am.

A: Well, it wouldn't surprise me. I've been reading about people like you.

S: What do you mean?

A: Well, I've heard that people are spending so much time on their computers that they develop some kind of personal attachment to them, as if they've made a new friend.

R: What – they start treating them as if they were human?

A: Yes, something like that. This article says that these people feel kind of depressed when they switch off. And they talk to their computer regularly. Do you do that, Sheryl?

S: Erm …

R: You do! I've heard you say good night to it.

S: Well, it's not as bad as people who are addicted to their mobile phones – Alex! I saw a programme on the telly about people actually changing the shape of their thumbs because they do so much texting.

R: Yeah, I saw that and it said that they're using their thumbs for other things that you usually do with your finger, like ringing doorbells and pointing.

A: Wow, I didn't see that but I did see something really interesting on that science programme. I thought it was a joke, but, apparently, they've brought out jeans that keep you young.

R: What kind of jeans are we talking about here?

A: Trousers – they come from Japan and they've got this enzyme in them that keeps the skin young.

S: No way!

A: No, really. Oh, what was it called? I can't remember, but basically, you just have to wear these jeans and you stay young and beautiful.

R: Hey, you'd better snap up a pair immediately, Sheryl. You need all the help you can get!

S: Look who's talking!

R: Seriously, though, I read something brilliant the other day. There's a company in California who've come up with a way of projecting enormous images onto the moon from the earth.

A: Come off it! How can they do that?

R: I think it said something about using satellites and huge lasers and mirrors – it's all very scientific, but they're going to show ads like on TV.

S: Well, I might be wrong, but I don't think you'll be able to see much, will you? It's too far away.

R: No, you'll be able to see it as clearly as you can see the moon. Just think about it, a giant logo smiling down on you.

S: What a stupid idea.

A: Actually, I think it's a brilliant idea. Just think how many people would see it.

S: But what will the man in the moon think?

 Listening script 20

Pronunciation and speaking Ex 2 from page 41

Unit 3 Money talks

 Listening script 21

Vocabulary and pronunciation Ex 3 from page 42

 Listening script 22

Reading text from page 43

 Listening script 23

(I = Interviewer; J = Joan; S = Sally; N = Nell)

I: Joan, let's start with you.

J: Oh yes, age before beauty.

I: Joan, do you think people have the same attitude to money now as you did when you were a young woman?

J: Well, I'm 67 now, so things have changed a lot since I was young. But I think the main difference is that I wouldn't dream of spending money I didn't have. I've never been a penny overdrawn at the bank, and I've never had a credit card. I wouldn't be able to sleep at night. But my daughter always seems to be overdrawn, and it doesn't bother her. Isn't that right, Sally?

S: Yes, Mum's right really. I do have credit cards, and I am in the red, but that's because things are so much more expensive nowadays.

I: And what about you, Nell. You're 23, and you've recently started your first job. Are you finding it hard to make ends meet?

N: Definitely – I mean, I'm not earning much yet and I'm paying back my student loan, so at the end of the month I'm always broke.

I: Sally, what does most of your money go on?

S: Food – feeding a family costs a fortune.

N: I go and eat at Mum's so that I can spend money on clothes. I've got a weakness for designer clothes without the bank balance to match.

J: You see that's another thing – we didn't have all this designer stuff. I made my own clothes! And I had one good handbag and one good pair of shoes. Not like these two – they have something new on every time I see them.

S: But one of the main differences between us is that I work and earn my own money, whereas you had to depend on an allowance from dad.

J: Yes, I was a housewife so I didn't have a salary. Women are much more independent financially nowadays and that's a good thing.

I: What advice would you give people about managing their finances?

J: Don't spend what you haven't got and always have something put by for a rainy day.

S: Mm, I think life's too short – you can't take it with you, so have a good time and enjoy it while you can.

J: I don't know how she turned out so irresponsible. I'm not mean, and I do treat myself to the odd luxury occasionally, but I do think you should be more careful, Sally.

S: I know, Mum, but I'm going to win the lottery, so I'm going be loaded.

I: Well, that's a good question to end on – how would each of you spend a million-pound lottery win?

J: Oh, I'd splash out on a world cruise – it's something I've always dreamt of.

S: I'd buy a little place in France and a private plane so I could go there every weekend.

N: I'd invest it.

J / S: What?

N: Ha ha … I'm only joking. I'd buy everything in Gucci.

Unit 4 I could kick myself

 Listening script 24

Reading text from page 47

 Listening script 25

Language study Ex 3 from page 48

 Listening script 26

Music extracts from page 49

 Listening script 27

(N = Nigel; E = Emma; T = Tarquin; P = Pablo)

N: Right, morning everybody.

E / T / P: Morning, Nigel.

N: So you've been working on the music for the five new TV commercials. Have you come up with some ideas?

T: Yah, we've chosen five tracks. We think they create the right associations with the products.

N: OK, let's start with the jeans. Emma?

E: Well, erm, we felt it was important to create the image of a hero, erm, the hero of a black and white movie – someone like James Dean or Marlon Brando.

N: Uh huh. Sounds good.

E: Soul music from the sixties always makes me think of old black and white movies, so I've chosen this one.

[music extract]

N: Yes, that's good. Everybody agree?

P: Yes, jeans are classic but they're still fashionable, so classic sixties music is perfect.

N: Right. Next is the family car – I think we need something that sounds happy and cheerful here.

T: Absolutely, so this is the kind of music that reminds me of family holidays when I was a kid.

[music extract]

N: Yeah, that's good. I like it. It reminds me of a very bad haircut I once had in the eighties. OK, olive oil?

E: Well, obviously, you associate olive oil with Italy, so it had to be opera. When I close my eyes and listen to this, I visualise Verona – amazing.

[music extract]

N: That's great, Emma. Now, the trainers are tricky. We want to attract the kids, but it's the parents who pay for them.

P: Well, we thought it was most important to attract fashionable young men. Hip hop sounds cool, so we chose this.

[music extract]

N: Yup, that's good – the parents won't like it, but they only have to pay. Is that it?

E: No, one more – the new perfume. It's called 'Amore'. This track takes me back to the most romantic evening I've ever had.

[music extract]

N: Yeah – I think that works well. OK, thanks, everybody. Emma, can you come into my office for a moment …?

Unit 5 Review

 Listening script 28

Part 1

Dan

It was my sister's 30th birthday, and I knew she was feeling old so I wanted to get her something that would make her feel better about being 30. I found the ideal thing – a foot spa. It's a gadget that massages your feet. You just put your feet in it and switch it on. Perfect – or so I thought.

Becky

My boyfriend had just got a new job and I wanted to give him something to say well done. He has to wear a suit for the new job so I decided to get him a tie – I found this trendy silk tie with Chinese symbols on it.

Greg

My girlfriend and I were going to get married and I got her a gold engagement ring with a big diamond in the middle. I knew she'd love it, but I wanted to find an original way of giving it to her. Anyway, I'd seen a film where the guy hides the ring in an ice cube and then serves it in a drink – such a cool idea.

 Listening script 29

Part 2

Dan

I could tell she wasn't impressed by the way she opened it. She looked at the box and didn't even get it out. Of course she said thank you and all that, but I found out later that she hated it and said it made her feel even older. I should have asked her what she wanted, then I wouldn't have made that mistake.

Becky

He liked the tie, or he said he liked it anyway. And it looked really good with his black suit, so I thought it was a success until he came back from work one day and said that he'd taken an important client for lunch in a Chinese restaurant. One of the waiters started laughing and told him that the letters on his tie meant 'this dish is cheap but very tasty'. He was so embarrassed. And the guy who sold me the tie in the shop was Chinese. If only I'd checked what it meant, but you don't really think about it, do you?

Greg

That evening, I put on some nice romantic music and got out the champagne. I told her it wasn't very cold so we needed ice, and she believed me. So, I carefully put the ice cube with the ring inside in her glass, and then the phone rang. It was her mother, and as usual they chatted for ages. Meanwhile, the piece of ice was getting smaller. Anyway, she finally came back into the room, and before I could say anything, she picked up her glass, took a big gulp and the ring went straight down her throat. It was stupid of me not to tell her. But if I'd told her, it would have spoilt the surprise. I wish I'd never had the stupid idea in the first place.

 Listening script 30

Song from page 52

Communication activities

Student B

Unit 2, Language study Ex 6 page 40

1 Match the phrasal verbs to the nouns.

A	try on	fill in	turn off	take off	give up	print out

B	a form	a shirt	smoking	the TV	a letter (on a computer)	your jacket

2 Listen to student A's sentences and respond using an appropriate phrasal verb from Ex 1 and the pronoun *it*. All the phrasal verbs are type 2 (must be separated by a pronoun).

Example:
A: *Do you think this shirt will fit me?*
B: *Try it on.*

3 Read your sentences to student A and listen to his / her responses. Does he / she give you sensible advice?

1 What shall I do with this wastepaper?
2 The music's too loud.
3 What shall I do with my homework?
4 What shall I do with my coat?
5 I don't know what this word means.
6 I'm too ill to have my party tonight.

Unit 2, Listening Ex 3 page 41

The hoax story was projecting advertisements onto the moon.

Module 3
Places

Unit	Topic	Language study	Vocabulary	Main skills
1 Life's a beach pages 66–69	• Island in the sun (The creation of an artificial island) • The world's best beach	• Passive and active	• Adjective + noun collocations • Expressions for recommending a place	• **Reading:** understanding numbers in a text; understanding key descriptions • **Listening:** checking the description of a procedure • **Speaking:** recommending a place • **Writing:** an email
2 The open road pages 70–73	• A cook's tour (A description of a stay in Portugal) • A life in travel (An interview with a traveller)	• Adjectives for describing a place	• Expressions associated with travel	• **Reading:** predicting and checking; understanding paragraph topics • **Listening:** understanding a description • **Speaking:** interviewing a partner about travel
3 Get a new life pages 74–77	• A new start (Relocating) • City profiles	• Talking about the future (present continuous, *going to, will, would like to, might, hope to*; future perfect and future continuous)	• Houses • City life • Ways of responding	• **Listening:** identifying key information; checking • **Speaking:** describing a house you would like to live in; responding naturally to news; discussing relocation • **Reading:** identifying key information; understanding vocabulary in context • **Writing:** a chatroom message
4 Going to extremes pages 78–81	• A test of endurance (A trip to extreme places) • Extreme living (Living in extreme conditions)	• Relative clauses • Omission of the relative pronoun	• Phrasal verbs • Extreme adjectives • Absolute adjectives	• **Reading:** identifying people and places; identifying key information; understanding vocabulary in context • **Speaking:** discussing survival and extreme places • **Listening:** predicting and checking • **Pronunciation:** sentence stress

1 Life's a beach

Island in the sun

Lead-in **1** Work with a partner. Only one of these photos shows a natural phenomenon. Which one do you think it is?

▲ Heart-shaped reef, Australia   ▲ Spiral Jetty, Utah   ▲ The Palm, Jumeirah, Dubai

Listening **1** 🖥 **01** Listen to the conversation between two friends, Petra and Ray. Answer these questions.

1 Which of the three places in the photos are they talking about?
2 How was Ray involved?   3 What is the place used for?

2 Look at the pictures which illustrate the construction of the Palm. Complete the procedure from memory. Then listen again and check your answers.

▲ Rocks and sand are brought from the (1) _____ and the (2) _____ is dropped into place. If all the materials were placed end to end, a (3) _____ could be built long enough to circle the world three times.

▲ Sand is sprayed into position and built up to the (4) _____ by a process called 'rainbowing'.

▲ A special geotextile sheet is laid on (5) _____ of the sand foundations to stop them from moving. Small rocks are lowered into place. The exact positioning is checked by (6) _____ .

▲ Over (7) _____ residents can be housed on the Palm. For visitors, the Palm offers 50 luxury hotels. Due to its scale and shape, the Palm can be seen from (8) _____.

'Sandcastles in the air' by Philip Jacoeson for *The Sunday Times Magazine*

3 The Palm has been described as the 'eighth wonder of the world'. Work with a partner and discuss these questions.

    1   What do you think of the Palm? Do you think it deserves to be the 'eighth wonder of the world'?

    2   What do you think are the most wonderful ancient and modern buildings in your country?

    3   Which buildings would you most like to visit in other parts of the world?

LANGUAGE STUDY

Passive and active

1 Look at these extracts about the Palm and answer the questions.

    a   *Rocks and sand **are brought** from the mainland.*

    b   ***They drop** the sand on the seabed.*

    c   *The exact positioning **is checked by** divers.*

    d   *The Palm **can be seen** from space.*

    1   Which of sentences a–d contain the passive?

    2   How is the passive formed? What is the auxiliary verb and the form of the main verb?

    3   How is the passive formed with modal verbs?

    4   Which of the passive sentences has an agent?

2 Match these explanations to extracts a–d in Ex 1.

    1   You use the passive <u>without</u> an agent when the person who does the action is unknown, unimportant, obvious or you don't want to identify him / her. ☐ ☐

    2   You use the passive <u>with</u> an agent when you want to place importance on who does the action. ☐

    3   In conversation, instead of using the passive without an agent, you can sometimes use the active with the subject *they, you*, etc. ☐

Grammar reference page 90

3 Complete the facts about the Palm with an appropriate passive form of the verbs in the box.

add	build	buy	choose	describe	expand	reach	use

    1   100 million cubic metres of sand _____ to build the Palm.

    2   The palm shape _____ because it maximises the beach area.

    3   Over 60 km _____ to Dubai's coastline by the creation of the island.

    4   The Palm can _____ by either boat, bridge or tunnel.

    5   Dubai International Airport _____ currently _____ to cope with the huge increase in visitors.

    6   Around 300 new hotels _____ by 2020 to accommodate visitors.

    7   When they first went on sale, a beach-front villa on the Palm could _____ and then re-sold the very next day for double the price.

    8   The Palm _____ recently _____ as the 'eighth wonder of the world'.

4 How might the information in Ex 3 be given in a conversation? Complete these sentences.

    1   They …   5   They …

    2   They …   6   They …

    3   The creation of the island …   7   When they first went on sale, you …

    4   You …   8   They …

5 Work with a partner. Student A turn to page 93 and student B turn to page 96.

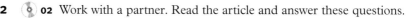

Reading and vocabulary

1 Work with a partner. Think about the best beach you have ever been to. What were the qualities that made it so good?

2 02 Work with a partner. Read the article and answer these questions.

1 What do these numbers refer to in the article?

14   20   26   37   1,000   86,000

2 What qualities did Pete Shannon look for in a beach? Were they the same as the qualities you discussed in Ex 1?

The world's best beach

Pete Shannon, 26, a graduate in computer science and marketing, was chosen from 1,000 hopefuls to undertake an eight-week trip round the world on behalf of internet company Expedia.

During those eight weeks, he travelled around 86,000 kilometres (the equivalent of more than twice round the equator), hopped on and off 37 planes, crossed 14 time zones and visited 20 beaches, to discover which sandy shoreline is worthy of the title 'World's Best Beach'.

'My criteria for the top beach was that it had to be clean, have good waves, be sunny all day with a light breeze and not be too crowded,' said Mr Shannon.

3 03 Read the web page on page 69, which shows Pete Shannon's top three beaches. Choose the sentence which best describes each place. There are two sentences you don't need.

1 It has a lake where you can swim with dolphins.
2 It's home to an Olympic swimmer.
3 It's surrounded by mountains.
4 It has a large coral reef.
5 It's completely surrounded by sand and water.

4 Work with a partner. Which of the top three beaches appeals most to you?

5 Read through the text again. Match these adjectives to the nouns they describe.

Example: crystal clear *water*

1 gentle   3 crunchy   5 twinkling   7 romantic
2 turquoise   4 secluded   6 tropical

6 Complete the phrases that Pete Shannon used with the words in the box. Then check your answers in the text.

see	check	struck	interested	Whatever	while	Watch

1 You're immediately _____ by ...
2 If you're _____ in ...
3 _____ out for ...
4 The best way to _____ away a couple of hours is ...
5 There is so much to _____ and do in ...
6 _____ you do, make sure you ...
7 And to finish off the day, _____ out ...

Speaking and writing

1 Think about a beach resort or other holiday destination you know. Make notes using the language in Ex 5–6. Recommend the place to a partner.

2 A close friend has emailed asking you to recommend a good place to go on holiday. Write back to your friend with your recommendation using your notes in Ex 1.

'The World's Best Beach Report' by Pete Shannon for *expedia.co.uk*

Home   Search   Shop   Bookmarks

3 Cancun, Mayan Coast, Mexico

You're immediately struck by the crystal clear water around Cancun. If you're interested in snorkelling or scuba diving, one of the world's largest barrier reefs lies off the coast. The grains of sand on the beach make for a very soft and comfortable day by the sea. There's often a gentle breeze along the coast and this helps to keep you cool in the sun – watch out for burning though!

2 Ihuru Island, Maldives

Wherever you are in the Maldives, you'll never be more than 20 metres away from the beautiful, light turquoise ocean. Ihuru Island is so small you can walk around it in 10 minutes. It's completely surrounded by gorgeous, crunchy sand. A typical day might include a spot of snorkelling or windsurfing in the morning, a lazy afternoon in the shade and a walk around the island before dinner.

The best way to while away a couple of hours after your evening meal is strolling along one of the secluded beaches, watching the twinkling lights on the distant sister islands and relaxing into the gentle Indian breeze.

And the winner is …

1 Waikiki Beach, Hawaii

If you like beaches to be busy but safe, and you like to know that all the usual fast food joints are just a short walk away, then this is the place for you.

There's so much to see and do on Waikiki. Whatever you do, make sure you hire a surf board from one of the famous 'Waikiki Beach Boys'. With Waikiki being home to the famous Duke Paoa Kahanamoku, the Hawaiian Olympic swimmer, lifesaver and man who introduced surfing to the world, there's no better place to hit the waves!

And to finish off the day in this tropical paradise, check out one of the hotel beach bars and watch the romantic sunset, drink in hand.

CD-ROM   For more activities go to **Places Unit 1**

2 The open road

LEARNING AIMS

- Can use adjectives for describing a place
- Can describe a scene from a window
- Can use travel vocabulary and discuss travel

A cook's tour

Lead-in **1** Work with a partner and discuss these questions.

1 What's your favourite foreign food? 2 Can you eat it in your town or city?

3 What local dish would you recommend to a foreign visitor in your country?

Reading **1** You are going to read a description of a stay in Portugal from Anthony Bourdain's book *A Cook's Tour*. Which of these phrases would you expect to see in the description? What kinds of places do the other phrases describe?

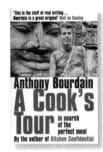

1 rows of leafless grapevines
2 palm trees swaying in the breeze
3 bright, flashing neon lights
4 grey sky over the valley
5 ancient Buddhist temples

6 a seventeenth-century inn
7 a concrete jungle of high-rise buildings
8 fields and orange groves
9 constantly burning wood fire
10 killer whales surfacing between icebergs

2 **04** Read the description and check your answers.

So it was with a mixture of excitement, curiosity, and dread that I woke up on a cold, misty morning in Portugal and looked out the window of my room at orderly rows of leafless grapevines, the fires from distant hearths issuing smoke into a gray sky over the valley. Where I was staying was a bed-and-breakfast, a seventeenth-century *quinta* (a private home turned country inn) about half a mile from the farm. It was set back from a twisting country road, past an arbor, surrounded by fields and orange groves and mountains, looking in every way as it must have four hundred years ago. Three young women looked after a few guests. There was a chapel, and a large dark country kitchen with a constantly burning wood fire and a long table. A vast carbon-blackened hooded chimney allowed most of the smoke to escape. The predominant smell in Portugal, I had quickly found, is wood smoke. The only source of heat in the large house – in my room, as well – was a burning fire. When I'd arrived late the previous night, there was one going in my room, creating a nice toasty zone, just large enough to undress and climb into the high four-poster bed.

'A Cook's Tour' by Anthony Bourdain, published by Bloomsbury Publishing Plc

3 Are these statements true or false?

1 Bourdain felt relaxed when he woke up. ☐

2 He could see the sea from his window. ☐

3 He was staying in a small family-run guesthouse. ☐

4 He felt as if the place had been frozen in time. ☐

5 The wood fire only heated a small part of his bedroom. ☐

4 In his description, Bourdain remembers the wood-smoke smell of Portugal. Think of different places you have visited. What are the predominant smells that you associate with them?

LANGUAGE STUDY

Adjectives for describing a place

1 Look back at the text on page 70 and find the adjectives which are formed from these words.

Adjectives from nouns: 1   mist   _____

2   leaf   _____

Adjectives from verbs: 3   twist   _____

4   blacken   _____

5   burn   _____

2 Work with a partner and answer these questions.

1 Which endings have been added to the nouns in Ex 1 for them to be used as adjectives? What is the difference in meaning between the two endings?

2 Which endings have been added to the verbs in Ex 1 for them to be used as adjectives? Which ending suggests movement or that the action is ongoing? Which ending suggests the result of an action?

Grammar reference page 90

3 Make adjectives from the words in **bold** to describe atmosphere / place.

nouns

1 a sky that has no **clouds**   a _____ sky

2 a landscape that has lots of **hills**   a _____ landscape

3 a coastline which is covered in **rocks**   a _____ coastline

4 a night on which the **moon** is obscured by cloud   a _____ night

5 a morning which is so cold there is **frost**   a _____ morning

verbs

6 a river which twists and **winds**   a _____ river

7 a street made of flat stones (**pave**)   a _____ street

8 a strong smell which **overpowers**   an _____ smell

9 a room which is full and untidy (**clutter**)   a _____ room

10 a busy and lively market (**bustle**)   a _____ market

4 Imagine that you have woken up in a different country and that you get up and look out of one of these windows. Make notes to answer these questions.

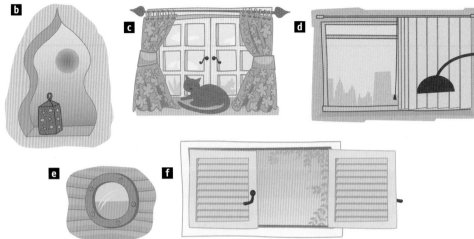

1 What is the weather like? (2 adjectives)

2 Which country / place are you in? (noun)

3 What can you see outside your window? (1 adjective + noun)

4 What does the sky look like? (2 adjectives)

5 What type of place are you staying in? (1 adjective + noun)

6 What is it surrounded by? (1 adjective + noun)

7 What can you see in the distance from your window? (2 adjectives + noun)

8 Open the window and breathe in. What can you smell? (1 adjective + noun)

5 Complete this description with your words in Ex 4.

> I woke up on a _____ morning in _____ and looked out of
> the window of my room at _____ and a _____ sky. Where I
> was staying was _____. It was surrounded by _____. In the
> distance I could see _____. The predominant smell was _____.

6 Work with a partner. Student A read your description aloud. Student B guess which window your partner was looking out of.

7 05 Listen to a description of the view through one of the windows. Which one is it?

A life in travel

Reading and speaking

1 06 Model and writer Laura Bailey was asked about her life in travel. Put the words of the interviewer's questions in the correct order. Then write the questions above each of the answers she gives on page 73.

a What's / best holiday / been / your / ?

b Are / or adrenalin junkie / a beach bum, / you / culture vulture / ?

c Who / be / ultimate travelling companion / your / would / ?

d Where / you / are / next / going / ?

e Where / spend / of your childhood / you / the summers / did / ?

f What / from your travels / you / have / learnt / ?

g Where / would / trip of a lifetime / be / your / ?

h What / read / you / on holiday / do / ?

i What / never travel / would / luxury / you / without / ?

'My Life in Travel' by Laura Bailey for *The Independent*

1 Where did you spend the summers of your childhood?

There was no real routine, but I do remember driving around Europe camping with my dad or staying in the south of France with my grandparents. We also rented little cottages in Devon and Cornwall or messed about on the river at home.

2 _____

I've got three, which I can't choose between because they were all so different: Parrot Cay in the Turks and Caicos for romance; Kenya for adventure; and New York, which I loved so much that I stayed there for five years, living in the West Village.

3 _____

Over the years I've learnt not to over-plan, to travel light and to stay open to adventure – sometimes a wrong turn can turn out to be a right turn. Also, a break close to home can be as relaxing as travelling long-haul – I'm a big fan of going to hotels in your home town.

4 _____

All three depending on mood and location.

5 _____

I read a real mixture of classics and modern novels as well as the odd fashion magazine. At the moment I'm doing a lot of research for a book but the last thing I read for pleasure was Claire Tomalin's biography of Samuel Pepys★.

6 _____

The boring answer would be my boyfriend. In my dream life I'd take Gabriel García Márquez to tell me stories, David Bailey to take pictures and the young Paul Newman to give me massages and feed me.

7 _____

My camera. I can't imagine going anywhere without it.

8 _____

I would really love to go to Sri Lanka and the Maldives. I want to scuba dive in the Maldives, but I'd like to do them both together. That's my dream at the moment.

9 _____

Harbour Island in the Bahamas for Easter.

Glossary ★Samuel Pepys = a 17th-century diarist from London

2 Match a word from A to words from B to make expressions. Then check your answers in the text.

A beach   travel   take   rent   trip   culture   adrenalin

B vulture   a cottage   junkie   pictures   of a lifetime   bum   light

3 Complete these sentences with the expressions in Ex 2.

1 For Yuko, the (a) _____ would be to go to Disneyworld in Florida.

2 Paula is such a (b) _____ – she loves to (c) _____ of important landmarks and learn something about the people and places she's visiting.

3 Sam finds it impossible to (d) _____, so he always takes much more than he needs.

4 Joe refuses to camp or even (e) _____; he prefers the luxury of a five-star hotel.

5 Anna and Steve are so different – he's a (f) _____, who loves sunbathing, while she's an (g) _____, who loves stuff like bungee jumping and paragliding.

4 Replace the names of the people in the descriptions in Ex 2 with the names of people you know to make true sentences. Then compare with a partner.

5 Think about how you would answer the questions in Ex 1. Then interview your partner using the questions.

CD-ROM   For more activities go to **Places Unit 2**

3 Get a new life

LEARNING AIMS

- Can use structures to talk about the future
- Can discuss city life and relocation
- Can respond naturally to news

A new start

Lead-in

1 Work with a partner. Would you ever consider living in a different country? Why / Why not? Discuss your ideas.

2 Work with a partner. Imagine you are choosing a new place to live. Tell each other what you would like using words from boxes A and B or your own ideas.

Example: *I just want to get away from the weather here.*

A	better	to be near	to get away from	lower	the same	bigger

B	the weather	friends and family	a city	the sea	crime levels
	cost of living	sports facilities	social life	language	
	food	house	garden	work opportunities	

Listening and vocabulary

1 ⊙ **07** Listen to the radio interview with Jem, a remedial masseur, talking about emigrating to Australia. Which of the subjects in Lead-in Ex 2 does he mention?

2 Use the words in the table to describe the place that Jem:

a is going to live in when he first arrives in Australia. b is hoping to buy later.

	small / large		a veranda
	wooden	house	a balcony overlooking the sea
	brick	flat	a thatched roof
A(n)	stone	bungalow with	a big garden and a barbecue
	one- / two-storey	cottage	wooden shutters
	old / modern	chalet	a swimming pool
			roses round the door

3 Work with a partner. What sort of house would you most like to live in? Use words in the table or your own ideas.

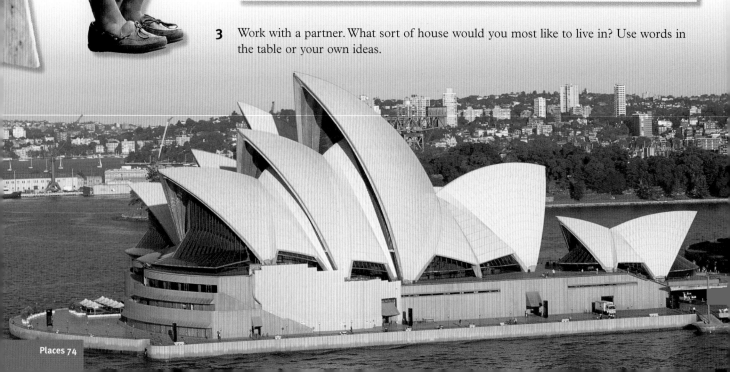

Ways of responding

Speaking **1** Complete these extracts from the interview with the words and phrases in the box using the information in brackets to help you. Then listen again and check your answers.

that sounds wonderful	Actually	I see what you mean	really	that's great

1 **Jem:** I'm going to move as soon as I get my visa and that can take up to 12 months.

Presenter: Oh, _____? That's longer than I thought. (shows you're surprised)

2 **Jem:** I'm a remedial masseur and the Australians are becoming more and more health-conscious, so massage is getting very popular there.

Presenter: Oh, _____. (shows you think this is a good thing)

3 **Jem:** In my profession it's essential to be able to communicate with my clients.

Presenter: Oh yes, _____. (shows you understand)

4 **Presenter:** You're not going to miss home at all, are you?

Jem: _____, there are lots of things I'll miss about the UK. (shows you are going to contradict)

5 **Jem:** So I'll get a bungalow with a nice big garden and a barbecue.

Presenter: Oh, _____. (shows you feel enthusiastic about a future plan)

2 Imagine you are relocating to a new city or country. Think about your answers to these questions and invent as many details as you like.

- Where are you going to relocate?
- Why have you chosen this place?
- What are you going to do there?
- Where are you going to live?
- What do you think you'll miss about home?

3 Work with a partner. Student A tell your partner about your new life. Student B use the words and phrases from Ex 1 to respond to your partner's news. Then swap roles.

LANGUAGE STUDY

Talking about the future

1 Look at these extracts from the listening activity. Match the verbs in **bold** to the uses a–d.

(1) *I'm going to move* as soon as I get my visa.

(2) *I'm flying over* to Australia next week just for three weeks to look at locations of where (3) *I'd like to live.* (4) *It'll probably be* on the north side of Sydney.

(5) *It might be* a shock if I moved to a country area where they're really conservative, but (6) *I'm hoping to be* very near Sydney.

(7) You*'re not going to miss* home at all, are you?

a a prediction or assumption 4 ☐ ☐

b a plan or intention ☐

c a firm arrangement ☐

d a desire ☐ ☐

Grammar reference page 90

2 Here are some responses to the question 'What are your hopes and plans for a better life?' Match the beginnings to the endings.

1 I might start   a   get my own place soon.
2 I'm definitely going to give up   b   smoking before my next birthday.
3 I'm hoping to   c   more optimistic about life.
4 As soon as I can,   d   yoga classes next week.
5 Things will be a lot better when   e   I've finished my studies.
6 I'm going to make more effort   f   taking a few more risks in life.
7 I'm starting   g   I'm going to have a holiday.
8 I'm going to try to be   h   to see my friends.

3 Think about your hopes and plans for a better life. Use the sentence beginnings in Ex 2 to write your 'good intentions'. Compare your ideas with a partner.

Example: *I'm definitely going to give up chocolate.*

Future perfect and future continuous

4 Look at this extract from the listening activity and answer the questions.

(1) *I'll **be staying*** with my brother and hopefully (2) *he'll **have found*** some information for me.

a   Which of the verbs in **bold** expresses:

something completed in the future? ☐

something in progress in the future? ☐

b   Which of the verbs in **bold** is an example of:

the future perfect? ☐

the future continuous? ☐

Grammar reference page 91

5 08 Complete Jem's answer to the question 'Where do you see yourself in ten years' time?' with the correct form of the verbs. Then listen and check your answers.

Hopefully, I (1 be) *'ll have been* in Australia for about nine years by then and I'd like to think that I (2 still / enjoy) _____ the things I enjoy now. In other words, I (3 go down) _____ to the beach regularly, I (4 play) _____ tennis every day and I (5 swim) _____ a lot. And with a bit of luck, I (6 set up) _____ my own practice, I (7 still / work) _____ and I (8 find) _____ a nice place to live.

6 Where do you see yourself in ten years' time? Think about what you'll be doing and what you'll have done. Compare your ideas with a partner.

Reading 1 09 After listening to the radio interview with Jem, Joel sent the message on page 77 to the radio station chat room. Read the message and find out:

1   where Joel lives.   4   his opinion of where he lives.
2   why he lives there.   5   his opinion of where he comes from.
3   where he comes from.   6   the solution suggested by Sally.

2 Replace the underlined words with words and phrases from Joel's message.

1   There's an incredible variety of things to do in the evening. (line 5)

2   I live away from the noisy activity of the city. (line 7)

3   You can spend hours walking slowly around the museums and art galleries. (line 11)

4   You can feel the age and culture of the place walking through the small roads and alleys. (line 13)

5   The streets are very busy until the early morning. (line 15)

3 Work with a partner. How many of the sentences in Ex 2 could describe where you live?

Discussion title: Oz to Oxford	Posted by	No of replies
I'm sure Jem'll have a great time and by this time next year he'll be lying on a beach wondering why it took him so long to make his move. Aussies are warm and friendly – he'll have no problem making friends. I did the opposite – moved from Sydney to Oxford in England and that 5 was difficult. Sydney is a fantastic city with an amazing nightlife. When I arrived in Oxford it was a shock – nobody seems to go out here, except to pubs, and they're so dark and smoky. I miss the hustle and bustle of the Sydney streets and I really miss the water – Oxford is as far as you can get from the coast – there's a river, but you can't exactly 10 surf on the Thames! Sydney's a really cool place – I really miss the live music there. Of course Oxford's not all bad – if you like strolling around museums and colleges. And the architecture's great and you can certainly soak up the history of the place just walking around the back streets, but everything stops at 11 pm! Every night in Sydney the 15 streets are buzzing into the small hours. And the weather – don't even get me started on that subject …!	Joel	1
You're obviously homesick, so why don't you just go home?	Sally	
My fiancée is from Oxford and she doesn't want to leave.	Joel	
So why don't you leave her? I like Australia … :-)	Sally	

Listening 1   🔟 **10** You are going to listen to part of a game show in which contestants can win a house in one of three places. Listen and write the names of the places mentioned.

2   Answer these questions from memory. Then listen again and check your answers.

Which of the places was described as:
1 Europe's coolest capital?   4 having a thriving art scene?
2 a city that never sleeps?   5 a cosmopolitan city?
3 a seriously vibrant place?   6 a really funky city?

In which place:
7 shouldn't you be afraid to haggle?   9 can you shop till you drop?
8 is getting around easy?

3   🔟 **11** The contestants had to answer a general knowledge question about each of the places in Ex 1. Listen to the questions and write an answer for each one.

4   🔟 **12** Listen to the answers to Ex 3 and find out if you too could win a house.

Writing 1   Imagine you have relocated to a new city. Write a chatroom message like Joel's saying what you miss about your city. Compare your new city with your home town.

CD-ROM   For more activities go to **Places Unit 3**

4 Going to extremes

LEARNING AIMS

- Can use relative clauses
- Can discuss extreme places
- Can understand absolute adjectives and sentence stress

A test of endurance

▲ Sahara Desert

Lead-in **1** Work with a partner. Match the words in the box to the environments shown in the photos.

> mosquitoes   camels   nomads   explorers
> tribes   caravan   kayaking   dust storm
> crocodiles   midnight sun   bows and arrows
> seal hunt

Reading and vocabulary **1** 🔊 **13** Read the preview of a new series of TV documentaries called *Going to more extremes* on page 79. Find out who or what the following are:

1	narwhal	3	Kombai	5	Agadez
2	Inuit	4	Tubu	6	Tuareg

▲ Arctic ice cap

2 Find the answers to these questions in the text.

1 Who does Nick <u>unexpectedly encounter</u> in Greenland? (line 4)

2 What local habit does Nick have to <u>tolerate</u> in Greenland? (line 10)

3 In Papua, what two creatures almost make Nick decide to <u>stop</u>? (line 24)

4 What helps him to change his mind and decide to <u>continue</u>? (line 26)

5 After his stay with the Tuareg, who does Nick <u>go</u> into the desert to try to find? (line 41)

6 Does Nick find it easy to <u>move at the same speed as</u> the women of the Tubu? (line 46)

▲ Tropical swamps of Papua New Guinea

3 Work with a partner. Replace the <u>underlined</u> words in Ex 2 with the phrasal verbs used in the text.

4 Complete these sentences so that they are true for you. Compare your ideas with a partner.

1 I sometimes find it difficult to keep up with …
2 I can put up with most things, but I can't put up with …
3 I'm going to carry on …
4 This weekend I'm going to head off to …
5 I want to give up …
6 The other day I came across …

Speaking

1 Match the sentence beginnings to the endings.

1 I'm not much good at braving
2 I've never suffered
3 I could endure any kind
4 I like to think that if I had to cross the Sahara, I could survive

a of extreme climate.
b the cold.
c the ordeal.
d from insomnia.

2 Work in small groups and discuss these questions.

1 Which of the sentences in Ex 1 are true for you?
2 Which of the three extreme situations described in the text do you think you would cope with best and worst?
3 Which areas in your country have the most extreme conditions?

Going to more extremes

An amazing new series from the National Geographic Channel

'Going to more extremes', published by The National Geographical Channel

Oxford Academic, Nick Middleton, tests his endurance.

Ice

Nick braves the continuous daylight of the Arctic ice cap in search of the mysterious narwhal, the rarely seen Arctic whale. The first person Nick comes across
5 on arrival in Greenland is a Norwegian explorer, rescued from the ice cap and looking very much the worse for wear. Nick decides he wants to avoid this fate, and sets off for training in ice survival and kayaking. Suffering from insomnia due to the
10 midnight sun, Nick has to put up with the locals' habit of hunting and eating anything that moves. Travelling north, he takes part in a seal hunt as preparation for an expedition with the Inuit, the indigenous people of the Arctic region, in search of
15 the elusive narwhal.

Swamp

Nick must wonder why he's come to Papua at all. Famous for its crocodile-infested swamps, the interior is inhabited by tribes notorious for headhunting and
20 cannibalism. What's more, despite his severe vertigo, Nick plans to meet the Kombai people, who live in houses 30 metres up in the trees. Having nearly been eaten alive by mosquitoes, and crocodiles too, he is ready to give up, but a short time in a surprisingly
25 'nice bit of swamp' gives him the energy he needs to carry on. However, on arrival at the Kombai village deep in the interior, his porters run away when three tribesmen with bows and arrows appear out of nowhere and surround him. Nick fears this situation
30 may, in fact, be too extreme to survive. And he wonders whether his preparations will protect him from the countless dangers he will face.

Sand

Nick travels to Niger, where he aims to cross the
35 Sahara with a caravan of women of the Tubu tribe. On arriving in the desert town of Agadez, Nick is hit by a dust storm raging out of the Sahara. He realises that he will need to learn a great deal about nomadic and desert life to survive his ordeal. He endures a
40 scalding bath and learns to race camels with the Tuareg, before heading off into the desert to try to locate the fearsome Tubu. After days of searching he finally finds the tribe, who hardly appear to deserve their reputation as some of the toughest women in
45 the world. Nevertheless, he doesn't find it so easy to keep up with them on the hardest section of their trans-Saharan journey.

LANGUAGE STUDY

Relative clauses

1 Look at the relative clauses in **bold** and answer the questions.
a   *Nick has to put up with the locals' habit of hunting and eating anything **that moves**.*
b   *Nick plans to meet the Kombai people, **who live in houses 30 metres up in the trees**.*
c   *Nick tries to locate the Tubu tribe, **which he finally manages after days of searching**.*
d   *When Nick is surrounded by tribesmen, the porters **that are accompanying him** flee into the jungle.*
e   *The Sahara Desert is the most arduous place **which Nick visits**.*

1   Which three of the relative clauses give essential information which tells us the exact thing we are talking about? (Defining relative clauses) [a] [ ] [ ]

2   Which two of the relative clauses give extra, non-essential information? (Non-defining relative clauses) [ ] [ ]

3   Which type of relative clause is separated from the main clause by a comma?

4   Which relative pronoun *(who, which* or *that)* refers to:
1   people?   2   things?   3   both people and things?

5   Which relative pronoun *(who, which* or *that)* <u>can't</u> be used in a non-defining relative clause?

Grammar reference page 91

2 Cross out any words that can't be used.

Example: I don't understand people ~~which~~ / *who* / *that* don't want to travel.

1   The climate *which* / *who* / *that* appeals to me most is warm and dry.
2   The world's largest city is Tokyo, *which* / *who* / *that* has about 30 million people.
3   I've got lots of friends *which* / *who* / *that* live in exotic places.
4   The thing *which* / *who* / *that* puts me off going to tropical places is the snakes.

Omission of the relative pronoun

3 You can omit the relative pronoun when the word following it is a subject (*he, Nick,* etc).
In which of these sentences can the relative pronoun be omitted?
1   *The country **which has** the most visitors is France.*
2   *The country **which I** would most like to visit is France.*

Grammar reference page 91

4 Delete the relative pronouns that can be omitted in these sentences. In which sentence is this not possible? Check your answers in the text on page 79.

1   The first person who Nick comes across … is a Norwegian explorer.
2   A short time in a surprisingly 'nice bit of swamp' gives him the energy which he needs to carry on.
3   And he wonders whether his preparations will protect him from the countless dangers that he will face.
4   After days of searching he finally finds the tribe, who hardly appear to deserve their reputation as some of the toughest women in the world.

5 Add any necessary relative pronouns to these sentences.

Examples: The most amazing place ____–____ I've ever been to is the Himalayas.
I'm not the kind of person ___*who*___ likes lying on the beach all day.

1   A country _____ I'd quite like to live in for a while is the USA.
2   People _____ do dangerous sports like bungee jumping must be crazy.
3   Trekking in the Amazon is something _____ I've always wanted to do.
4   I can't stand beach resorts _____ have lots of loud bars and discos.
5   The extreme place _____ I'd most like to visit is the Antarctic.

6 Change the sentences in Ex 5 to make them true for you.

Extreme living

Listening and vocabulary

1 🔘 **14** You are going to listen to five people talking about living in extreme places. Match the conditions to the places. Listen and check your answers.

1 the hottest   2 the lightest   3 the driest   4 the most crowded   5 the coldest

a Yukutia,
Eastern Siberia

b Mong Kok,
Hong Kong

c Mali,
West Africa

d Atacama Desert,
Chile

e Reykjavik,
Iceland

▲ Erin   ▲ Jamie   ▲ Lisa   ▲ Arturo   ▲ Halldora

2 Replace the underlined words in these sentences with the words and phrases in the box.

> gigantic   sky-high   packed with   deserted   boiling   minuscule
> rock-bottom   freezing

1 In winter the streets are <u>empty</u>.
2 The streets are <u>full of</u> people dancing.
3 Rents are <u>really expensive</u>.
4 You can get water underground but that only accounts for a <u>very small</u> percentage of the water we need.
5 After a few minutes outside in the <u>extremely cold</u> temperatures, your nostrils fill with ice.
6 It's <u>extremely hot</u> even in the shade.
7 They're building a <u>massive</u> observatory on top of a mountain.
8 Temperatures reach <u>the lowest point possible</u>.

3 Which places do the sentences in Ex 2 refer to? Listen again and check your answers.

4 Put the words in the box in Ex 2 into pairs of opposites.

Absolute adjectives

Pronunciation and speaking

1 🔘 **15** Listen to Hannah and her teenage son talking to a friend about their weekend away. <u>Underline</u> the stressed syllables in Hannah's responses.

	Friend	**Sam**	**Hannah**
1	How was your weekend?	All right.	Fantastic! We had a <u>fabulous</u> time.
2	Oh good. And the weather?	Not bad.	The weather was absolutely perfect.
3	Wow. I bet it was hot.	Yeah, quite hot.	It was boiling.
4	So, you went swimming then?	No, the water was a bit cold.	The water was absolutely freezing!
5	Were there many people on the beach?	Yeah, quite a few.	The beach was packed.
6	Did you find a nice restaurant?	Not really.	Yes, we found a brilliant place.
7	How was your meal?	OK.	It was delicious.
8	What about the journey back?	Not bad.	Great – the roads were deserted.

2 Work in groups of three. Act out the dialogue in Ex 1.

3 Choose one of the topics below and write five questions about it. Then work in groups of three. Take it in turns to ask the questions, and to play the teenager and the mother.

> a film   a party   a city   a meal   a football match   a concert

CD-ROM   For more activities go to **Places Unit 4**

Lead-in   **1** Combine words from boxes A and B to make six famous London places. Add any more landmarks that you know.

A	Trafalgar the British Wembley Covent the West the London

B	Garden End Square Eye Museum Stadium

Home is where the heart is

1 🔊 **16** Listen to an interview with London-based musician Tom Kenny. Match the places in Lead-in Ex 1 to these questions.

1 Where do you live and why?
2 What's your favourite place in London?
3 And your least favourite?
4 What's your idea of a perfect Friday night?
5 Where would you want to be taken on a date?
6 What's the first piece of advice you'd give to a tourist?

2 What does Tom describe using these words? Listen again and check.
1 vibrant   2 packed   3 soulless   4 buzzing   5 funky   6 romantic
7 deserted   8 cool

3 Work with a partner and ask and answer the questions in Ex 1 about where you live.

4 Choose the correct relative pronoun in these extracts. Check in listening script 16 on page 85. In which sentence can the relative pronoun be omitted?

1 Tom, *who / that* plays guitar with up-and-coming pop band, The Change, is a true London aficionado.
2 I live in Covent Garden, *which / that* is a really happening part of the city.
3 The West End has loads of funky little back-street clubs *who / that* have live music.
4 It's one of the most romantic things *who / that* you can do.

5 Complete the sentences about your home town or city with a relative clause. Discuss your ideas with a partner.

1 There's a really good club in town
2 I love going to places
3 I like to go out with people   } which / that / who …
4 I hate places
5 I'd love to live somewhere

A new start

1 Choose the more appropriate alternatives.

House and contents up for auction

A six-storey house along with the entire contents (1) *is being auctioned / ~~will have been auctioned~~* next week because its owner, William Thomas, 56, (2) *is starting / will start* a new life in southern Italy, taking only one suitcase of possessions with him. 'I (3) *'ll have started off / 'm going to start off* ' with just the bare essentials and I (4) *'m trying / 'm going to try* to buy only the things I absolutely need,' Mr Thomas told would-be buyers as they viewed the house in Oxford, UK. 'All being well, by this time next week, I (5) *'ll get rid of / 'll have got rid of* everything, except for the things in the suitcase of course, and with a bit of luck a month from now I (6) *'ll be enjoying / 'll have enjoyed* a clutter-free existence in my new home in Italy.' Mr Thomas is hoping that the contents, which includes antiques and paintings, (7) *are making / will make* at least £1 million and that the house itself (8) *will sell / will be selling* for around £3 million. Mr Thomas wouldn't reveal the contents of his suitcase.

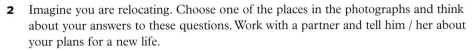

2 Imagine you are relocating. Choose one of the places in the photographs and think about your answers to these questions. Work with a partner and tell him / her about your plans for a new life.

- Where are you moving to?
- Why does this place appeal to you?
- What is your new home like – inside and the surroundings?
- What are you going to take with you?
- What are you going to do in your new home – for work, socialising, sport and leisure activities, etc?

- What kind of people do you think you'll meet?
- What will you miss from home?
- What will you be doing a year from now?
- What will be the pros and cons?

Rearrange your home – energise your life

1 Read and respond to the statements in the questionnaire. Then calculate your score.

---

a Yes, absolutely. **b** Yes, sort of. **c** No, not really. **d** No, definitely not.

1 The entrance to my house is spacious, inviting and clean. _____
2 I've kept some photos and mementos even though they have negative associations. _____
3 There is space in my home for new things. _____
4 I have pictures lying around that need to be hung on the walls. _____
5 My home is well lit in every room. _____
6 My bedroom is messy and cluttered. _____
7 I have books on display in my home. _____
8 The windows in my home need cleaning. _____

How to score
Statements 1, 3, 5, 7: a = 3 / b = 2 / c = 1 / d = 0   Statements 2, 4, 6, 8: a = 0 / b = 1 / c = 2 / d = 3

---

2 Complete the 'What it means' section with the correct passive form of the verbs. Then check what your score means. Is this an accurate description of your home?

What it means

17–24 points: Your home (1 design) *has been designed* for maximum energy flow. The rooms (2 organise) _____ so that they are light and uncluttered and all the things that prevent energy flow (3 eliminate) _____ . Well done, you must be bursting with energy.

8–16 points: You're doing a lot of the right things, but the energy flow in your home could (4 improve) *be improved*. Things that are holding negative energy need (5 eliminate) _____: pictures should (6 hang up) _____ and old letters and photos that (7 associate) _____ with negative feelings should (8 burn) _____ . Once this (9 do) _____ , you'll find your energy levels increasing.

0–7 points: The energy flow in your home (10 prevent) *is being prevented* by a number of things. But if you follow a few simple steps, everything can (11 put) _____ right very easily: broken things should (12 throw away) _____ or fixed, anything that (13 not use) _____ needs putting away in a cupboard. And make sure your home is as light as possible – windows should (14 clean) _____ and light bulbs replaced. Do these few things and your life (15 transform) _____ .

Song

1 Read the factfile about the band Keane and answer these questions.

1 When did Keane get together?   3 Who released their first singles?

2 What music did the band originally play?   4 How did they get their big break?

factfile

British band Keane was formed in 1997 by childhood friends Tom Chaplin (vocals), Richard Hughes (drums) and Tim Rice-Oxley (piano). Keane started out as a cover band, playing mainly U2 and Beatles songs, but they got tired of playing other people's songs and in 1999 they began writing and recording their own material. Their first singles were released independently in 2000 and 2001, but record labels were slow to recognise their talent. They got their big break in December 2002 when a record company executive was so impressed by one of their gigs that he offered to release their next single, *Everything's changing*. This was a huge success on radio, their reputation grew and soon the band were playing in their first UK tour. In the autumn of 2003 they signed a record deal and their debut album, *Hopes and fears*, which includes the song *Somewhere only we know*, was released in 2004.

2 🔘 **17** Listen to the song and choose the correct alternative in each line.

Somewhere only we know

I walked across an empty *space / land / room*
I knew the pathway like the *back / palm / fingers* of my hand
I felt the earth *between / under / beneath* my feet
Sat by the river and it made me *sleep / complete / wet*

Chorus

Oh simple *life / thing / mind*, where have you gone?
I'm getting old and I need something to *go / lean / rely* on
So tell me when you're gonna let me *in / down / through*
I'm getting tired and I need somewhere to *live / sleep / begin*

I came across a *leafless / fallen / twisted* tree
I felt the branches of it *looking / smiling / pointing* at me
Is this the *place / time / one* we used to love?
Is this the place that I've been *speaking / singing / dreaming* of?

Chorus

So if you have a *minute / chance / heart* why don't we go
Think / Talk / Laugh about it somewhere only we know?
This could be the end of *love / life / everything*
So why don't we go somewhere only we know?

Repeat chorus and verse 3

3 Listen to the song again and read the lyrics. Discuss these questions with a partner.

1 Who is he talking to?   3 Where does he want to go? Why?

2 How is he feeling?

4 Spend a few minutes thinking about a place which is or was special to you. Tell your partner about it.

30-second places

1   Read how to play '30-second places' and play the game.

How to play

1   Play in groups of three to five. Each group needs a dice and each player needs a counter. All the players put their counter on the 'start' square.

2   Player 1 rolls the dice and moves the appropriate number of squares. If he / she lands on a 'TALK ABOUT' square, he / she must talk about the place for 30 seconds. Players should be timed from the moment they start talking to give them some thinking time.

3   If he / she lands on an 'ASK ANYBODY IN THE GROUP' square, he / she should read the topic aloud to the relevant player, who then talks about the topic for 30 seconds.

4   If a player has nothing to say on the topic they have landed on, they are allowed to pass and miss a turn, but they can only do this once in the game.

5   The game continues until the first player reaches the 'finish' square.

start

1 TALK ABOUT a place where you can shop 'til you drop

2 TALK ABOUT a place which is very cosmopolitan

3 TALK ABOUT a place that has interesting back streets

7 TALK ABOUT a place where prices are sky-high or rock-bottom

6 TALK ABOUT a place with crystal clear waters

5 ASK ANYBODY IN THE GROUP about their favourite landscape

4 TALK ABOUT your favourite place to while away a few hours

8 TALK ABOUT a place which is boiling or freezing

9 TALK ABOUT a place which was or would be the trip of a lifetime

10 ASK ANYBODY IN THE GROUP about a place they're hoping to visit one day

11 TALK ABOUT a place which has great nightlife

15 ASK ANYBODY IN THE GROUP about a place where they spent childhood holidays

14 TALK ABOUT a place where you enjoy doing sport

13 TALK ABOUT a place where you've watched a romantic sunset

12 TALK ABOUT a place where you can soak up the history

16 TALK ABOUT a place that you often head off to at the weekend

17 TALK ABOUT a place with a great view

18 TALK ABOUT a place which is perfect for sunbathing

finish

Extra practice

Unit 1

1 Put the words in brackets in the correct order to complete the sentences.

1 There's (see / much / so / to / do / and) _____
_____ in Thailand.

2 (immediately / You're / by / struck) _____
_____
the hustle and bustle of the place.

3 A (to / great / place / away / while) _____
_____ a couple of hours
is Khao San Road in Bangkok.

4 (off / day / finish / the / To) _____
_____ you could have
dinner while watching the sunset over the river.

5 (in / interested / you're / If) _____
_____ temples, you'll
be spoilt for choice throughout the country.

6 And (check out / whatever / do / you) _____
_____
the beaches in the south of the country.

2 Complete the email with the words in the box.

| breeze | clear | mainland | sandy | secluded |
| sunset | waves | turquoise | twinkling | |

New Message

To: Elena@yahoo.com
Cc:
Subject: The perfect beach

Hi Elena

Well, we finally made it to the beach and what
a wonderful place it is. The only way to get here
is by boat, which means it's really quiet and
(1) _____. The sea is a lovely
(2) _____ colour and crystal
(3) _____ with a (4) _____
bottom. And the water is so warm with really
gentle (5) _____ – perfect for swimming,
which is about all we do here! It's hot and there
isn't a cloud in sight – but there's a lovely, gentle
(6) _____ to keep us cool. At the end of
the day, everybody sits on the beach to watch
the (7) _____
and then it's dinner while watching the
(8) _____ lights on the (9) _____
across the sea. Life doesn't get much better
than this! See you in a couple of weeks.

Love
Kalina x

3 Write an e-postcard describing a beach you have been to.

4 Complete these facts about beaches with the correct passive form of the verbs in box A. Guess the correct numbers from box B. (Check your answers on page 96.)

| A | build | estimate | heat | open | visit | win |

| B | 2002 | 1995 | 85 | 1 million | 2,000 |
| | 600 billion billion | | | | |

1 The world's largest indoor beach is at Ocean
Dome water park in Japan, which
_____ in 1993. It is _____
metres long.

2 The world's busiest beach is Haeundae Beach in
South Korea. It _____ by up to
_____ people each day.

3 The first beach football World Championship
_____ by Brazil in _____.

4 Every summer since _____, an artificial
beach _____ along a stretch of the banks
of the River Seine in Paris.

5 To make sand into glass, it must _____
to at least _____ °C.

6 It _____ that there are _____
grains of sand on the earth's beaches.

5 Rewrite the underlined extracts from a travel brochure as they might be given in a conversation.

If it's tropical paradise and luxurious seclusion
you want, then the 1,200 islands of the Maldives
is a must. The Maldivians can't be beaten for
natural grace and charm, and hospitality and
good humour is second nature. Strict planning
laws mean that (1) only one hotel has been built
on each island, which gives the feeling of being
on your very own private island. (2) Fine
powdery sand, a turquoise sea and swaying palm
trees will be found wherever you wander and
(3) year-round sunshine is guaranteed. And
should you want a few days' away from island
life, (4) trips to nearby Sri Lanka and Dubai can
be organised to suit your needs. (5) An all-
inclusive week-long stay on the Maldives can be
booked for as little as £1,000.

Example: The brochure says you *can't beat the Maldivians for natural grace and charm.*

1 Apparently, they _____
2 It says you _____
3 They _____
4 Apparently, they _____
5 According to the brochure, you _____
_____

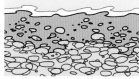

Unit 2

1 Complete the questionnaire with the words in the box. Then do the questionnaire and find out what kind of traveller you are.

> camping   lifetime   cruise   sunbathing
> trips   five-star   landmarks   sights
> travel light   renting

Questionnaire

1 When you're travelling or on holiday, do you prefer
a to see all the (1) _____ ?
b to take things slowly day by day?
c non-stop action?
d organised (2) _____ and tours?

2 Which kind of holiday accommodation do you prefer?
a a small, family-run hotel
b (3) _____ a beach hut
c (4) _____ under the stars
d a (5) _____ hotel

3 How do you like to eat on holiday?
a a local restaurant
b fresh pineapple or mango
c something high in carbohydrates
d room service

4 Which of these outdoor activities most appeals to you?
a coffee in a pavement café
b (6) _____ and lazing on the beach
c snowboarding
d a glass of wine in the jacuzzi

5 What items do you always take with you on holiday?
a a guidebook – I like to know what I'm looking at
b just shades and suncream – I like to (7) _____
c my first-aid kit – I never leave home without it
d matching suitcases – full of several coordinated outfits

6 What's your trip of a (8) _____ ?
a a tour of Europe's famous (9) _____
b backpacking around south-east Asia
c surfing in Australia
d a Caribbean (10) _____

What it means
Mostly As: Culture vulture. You love finding out what makes people and places tick.
Mostly Bs: Beach bum. You like to relax and take each day as it comes. You like your company cool and your water warm.
Mostly Cs: Adrenalin junkie. You are full of energy and love to be on the move to find new challenges and experiences.
Mostly Ds: Planned and pampered. You love to be looked after and going on holiday is the perfect way to indulge yourself.

2 Add -y or -less to the nouns in the box to describe each picture.

> window   pebble   rain   mist   cloud

1 a _____ day   2 a _____ room   3 a _____ sky

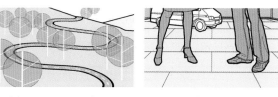

4 a _____ morning   5 a _____ beach

3 Use the -ing or -ed form of the verbs in the box to describe each picture.

> clutter   tire   pave   wind

1 a _____ road   2 a _____ square

3 a _____ desk   4 a _____ walk

4 Complete these descriptions of famous landmarks by adding -ed or -ing. Can you name the landmarks?

1 A half-human, half-lion ancient Egyptian statue symbolis_____ strength and wisdom.

2 A 650-year-old Italian bell tower lean_____ to one side.

3 An awe-inspir_____ Indian tomb with jewel-encrust_____ walls situated at the end of a beautiful garden.

4 An impos_____ grey figure with outstretch_____ arms dominat_____ the Rio skyline.

5 An unusually-shap_____ white building, with a strange-look_____, point_____ roof overlook_____ Sydney harbour.

Unit 3

1 Complete the email with the words and phrases in the box.

> get around   soaking   get away from
> buzzing   cosmopolitan   drop   hustle
> nightlife   sleeps   strolling

```
 ○○○                  New Message                    ○
      To:  katiem@hotmail.com
      Cc:
   Subject:  At home in NYC
```

Hi Katie

I've been here in my new home in NYC for a
few days now. My job doesn't start until next
week, so I've been spending the days (1) _____
around and seeing the sights. It's great just
(2) _____ up the atmosphere of the place.
Manhattan's not actually that big and it's quite
easy to (3) _____ on foot. It's really (4) _____,
with people from just about every country and
culture you can imagine.
The streets are (5) _____ with people and
there's something going on round every corner.
And if the (6) _____ and bustle gets too much,
you can always spend a few hours walking in
Central Park – a great place to (7) _____ it all.
And of course I've been checking out the
(8) _____. There are some great pubs, bars and
clubs – it sure is the city that never (9) _____.
Anyway, you must come over and visit. And
bring your credit card – it's the perfect place to
shop til you (10) _____ and the prices are
pretty good compared with home. You'd love
it. I'll write again soon.

Love
Andy x

---

2 A friend wants to know about your town or city.
Write a brief email describing the city / town / village
life of where you live. Use as many of the words and
phrases from Ex 1 as you can.

3 Are these words a type of house, a feature of a house,
or a material? Write T, F or M.

storey ☐   veranda ☐   brick ☐   bungalow ☐

wood ☐   cottage ☐   stone ☐   flat ☐

shutters ☐   balcony ☐   chalet ☐   roof ☐

4 Complete this dialogue with the words in the box.

> actually   sounds   mean   really   great

A: We've found an apartment at last.

B: (1) _____? That's (2) _____.
Where is it?

A: (3) _____, it's one of those new
apartments, you know, the ones overlooking the
river. It's got an amazing view of the city.

B: Lucky you! It (4) _____ wonderful.
When are you moving in?

A: Not for a while. Here, look at this photo. As you
can see, there's still a bit to be done before we
move in.

B: Yes, I see what you (5) _____. So, no
housewarming party for a few months, then?

5 Choose the most appropriate alternatives in this
conversation.

Ali: We (1) *'ll get / 're getting* out of here and we
(2) *will have spent / 're spending* the winter in
India this year.

Ben: Lucky you! When (3) *will you go / are you
going*?

Ali: In January. We (4) *'ll go / 're going* for three
months altogether.

Ben: Nice, what (5) *are you going to do / are you
going to have done* over there?

Ali: No, real plans. It (6) *'s just being / 'll just be*
great to get away from the winter. I guess we
(7) *'ll spend / are spending* a bit of time in
Delhi and then we (8) *'ll probably head / are
probably heading* down south to some of the
beaches.

Ben: Have you already got places to stay or (9) *are
you looking / are you going to look* for
something when you get there?

Ali: No, we (10) *'re going to find / 're finding* places
as we go. I don't think we (11) *'re having / 'll
have* any trouble – apparently there are loads
of cheap hotels.

Ben: Sounds like you (12) *'re going to have / 're
having* a great time. And I guess while I'm
struggling to work in the ice and snow, you
(13) *'ll lie / 'll be lying* on a beach somewhere
enjoying the sun.

Ali: Well, if all goes to plan, that's exactly what we
(14) *'ll be doing / 'll have done*.

Ben: And when did you say you (15) *'ll come / 're
coming* back?

Ali: Some time in April. I'm sure we (16) *'ll be
having / 'll have had* enough sun, sea and sand
by then!

Unit 4

1 Complete this extract from an online brochure with *who*, *which* or *that*. If the relative pronoun can be omitted, leave the space blank.

COUNTDOWN

You will be picked up in the Virgin Galactic executive jet and taken to the Virgin Galactic luxury space resort, (1) _____ will be your home for the next six days.

Every morning you will travel by helicopter to the spaceport, (2) _____ provides you with training and medical preparation. There are many space experts on hand, (3) _____ will be there to help you get the most from your experience.

LIFT-OFF

5, 4, 3, 2, 1 … the journey (4) _____ will take you into space begins. At an altitude of 16 km your spaceship, (5) _____ has so far been carried by a mothership, is released. The rockets fire and you then accelerate to a speed faster than a bullet.

The familiar blue sky (6) _____ you have been travelling through will turn to mauve and indigo and finally black. Out will come the stars, (7) _____ will be clearer and brighter than ever.

Soon the rocket engine cuts out and everything is quiet. You are weightless. You are in space.

Your astronaut pilot, (8) _____ will be more than happy to answer your questions, will manoeuvre the spacecraft so you can look back at the planet (9) _____ you have just come from. It will be the most exhilarating few minutes (10) _____ you have ever experienced.

TOUCHDOWN

After these precious minutes soaking up the thrill of space, an experience (11) _____ you will be able share with only a very few, you will start your return to earth. You will then land back at the spaceport after an experience (12) _____ is simply out of this world.

2 Write two responses for each question with *absolutely* and the adjectives in the box.

> boiling   delicious   deserted   ~~fantastic~~   freezing
> disgusting   packed   rock-bottom   sky-high
> ~~terrible~~

Example: *So, how was your trip?*

a *Absolutely fantastic.* **b** *Absolutely terrible.*

1 How was the weather?

a _____ b _____

2 Was it busy?

a _____ b _____

3 How was the food?

a _____ b _____

4 And the prices?

a _____ b _____

3 Write five sentences about places you have been to using the adjectives in Ex 2.

Example: *The beaches are packed in Greece in summer.*

_____

_____

_____

_____

_____

4 Complete the sentences with the correct form of the phrasal verbs in the box.

> keep up with   put up with   head off
> come across   give up   carry on

1 I'm going to _____ studying English after this course.

2 The other day, I _____ an old CD I thought I'd lost.

3 I _____ always _____ new fashions ever since I was a teenager.

4 Most weekends I enjoy _____ to the beach with my friends.

5 By the beginning of January next year, I _____ smoking.

6 I couldn't _____ the noise in the hotel and so I complained to the manager.

Grammar reference

Unit 1

Passive and active

Form

General tenses

| the appropriate tense of *be*, eg *is* / *was* / *has been*, etc | past participle |

Modal verbs

| *can* / *might*, etc | *be* | past participle |

Use

You use the passive when the new or important information is what happens to someone or something and not what someone or something does:
*The sand **was dropped** on the seabed. The island **was built** up gradually.*
*The flight **has been delayed**.*
*He's **going to be promoted**.*

The 'agent' is the person who does the action. You use the passive without an agent when the person who does the action is unknown, unimportant, obvious or you don't want to identify him / her:
*The Palm Jumeirah **can be seen** from space.*
*My passport **has been stolen**.*

You can use the passive with *by* + agent when you want to place importance on who does the action. This is often when the 'who' is the new, added information:
*The Palm project is a new luxury resort. It **was conceived by** Sheikh Mohammed bin Rashid Al Maktoum.*

In speech, instead of using the passive you often use the active. If there is no agent, you can use the subject *they, you, someone, people,* etc:
*Is it true **you can see** the Great Wall of China from space?*
*Someone **has stolen** my bike.*

Unit 2

Adjectives for describing a place

Descriptions can be made more vivid and atmospheric by using adjectives and participles. You can sometimes form adjectives from nouns and verbs.

Adjectives

Adjectives usually come before the noun they are describing or after noun / pronoun + *be*:
*I could see **orderly** rows of **leafless** grapevines.*
*There was a **bustling** market.*
*The room was very **crowded**.*

Adjectives from nouns

You can change some nouns into adjectives by adding the suffixes *-y* and *-less*:

– noun + *-y* to give the meaning 'having':
*I woke up on a **misty** morning.*
*Their new apartment is very **roomy**.*

– noun + *-less* to give the meaning 'not having':
*We stayed in a **windowless** room.*
*The **featureless** landscape stretched for miles.*
*The bus was hot and **airless**.*

Verbs as adjectives

You can use the present and past participles of some verbs as adjectives.

The present participle describes activity or movement:
*A **constantly-burning** fire heated the room.*
*There was an **overpowering** smell of garlic.*
*The **winding** road disappeared into the distance.*

The past participle describes the result of an action:
*It had a **carbon-blackened** chimney.*
*There's a **recently-built** shopping centre next to the hotel.*
*There were several **broken** windows.*
*The food was **overcooked**.*

Nouns as adjectives

You can use some nouns as adjectives to define the noun they are describing. These are sometimes called 'defining nouns':

| a **country** road | a **four-poster** bed |
| a **wood** fire | a **coffee** shop |

Participle clauses

A participle clause consists of a present or past participle + noun phrase. Participle clauses come after the noun they are describing:
*I was staying in a farm **surrounded by fields**.*
*There was a fire **going in my room**.*
*There was a small door **leading to a lovely garden**.*

Unit 3

Talking about the future

The three most common forms for talking about the future are *will, going to* and the present continuous.

will

You use *will* to talk about assumptions, predictions and opinions:
*How different do you think your life **will** be in Australia?*
*There are lots of things I'**ll** miss about England.*
*It **won't** be easy.*

You can also use other modal verbs such as *might, may* and *could* in this way:
*We **might** go to Spain later this year.*

going to

You use *going to* + infinitive to talk about plans and intentions made before the moment of speaking:
I'm going to move as soon as I get my visa.
What are you going to tell him?

You can also use *going to* + infinitive to express a prediction that is based on present or past evidence:
You're not going to miss home at all, are you?
It looks like it's going to be a nice day.

Present continuous

You use the present continuous to talk about firm arrangements made before the moment of speaking:
I'm flying over to Australia for three weeks.
We're going to Greece this summer.
What time are we meeting tomorrow?

want / would like / hope, etc

You can use verbs such as *want, would like, hope*, etc to express desires about the future:
When are you hoping to move to Australia?
We'd really like to live abroad for a few years.

Future continuous

Form

will / won't	be	-ing

Use

You use the future continuous to talk about something in progress at a specific time in the future:
I'll be staying with my brother next week.
I'll be lying on a beach this time tomorrow.

Future perfect

Form

will / won't	have	past participle

Use

You use the future perfect to talk about something which happened before a specific time in the future:
Hopefully, I'll have been in Australia for about nine years by then.
When do you think you'll have finished the report?

when / after / before / as soon as, etc

After adverbials such as *when, after, before, as soon as*, etc you use either the present simple or the present perfect when referring to the future. The present perfect emphasises the completion of an event or action:
I'll call you as soon as we arrive.
I'm hoping to go on holiday when I've finished my exams.

Unit 4
Relative clauses

Relative clauses describe or provide information about someone or something already mentioned.

Defining relative clauses

Defining relative clauses give essential information. They define the person or thing you are talking about.

You use *who* or *that* for people, *which* or *that* for things and *whose* for possession:
I don't understand people who just stay by the hotel pool all day.
There's a restaurant round the corner that does pizza.
That's the guy whose party we're going to tomorrow.

Non-defining relative clauses

Non-defining relative clauses give extra, non-essential information about the person or thing you are talking about.

You use *who* for people, *which* for things and *whose* for possession. You cannot use *that* in a non-defining relative clause.

Non-defining relative clauses are separated from the main clause by commas.

Non-defining relative clauses are more common in formal and written English:
The Atacama Desert, which has had rain only once in 400 years, is the driest place on earth
The company is based in Birmingham, which is the UK's second biggest city.

Omission of the relative pronoun

You can sometimes omit the relative pronoun in defining relative clauses. It cannot be omitted in non-defining relative clauses.

When the relative pronoun is followed by a subject, you can omit the relative pronoun:
The tickets that you sent off for have arrived. or *The tickets you sent off for have arrived.*

The omission of relative pronouns is more common in speaking than in writing and only when the sentence is short and simple.

Wordlist

Unit 1

accommodate *v* /ə'kɒmədeɪt/ *
barrier reef *n* /ˌbæriə 'riːf/
be interested in *phrase* /bi 'ɪntrəstɪd ˌɪn/
be struck by *phrase* /ˌbi 'strʌk ˌbaɪ/
beach *n* /biːtʃ/ ***
beach-front *adj* /'biːtʃˌfrʌnt/
book (a seat) *v* /bʊk ('ə siːt)/ **
breeze *n* /briːz/ **
check out *v* /ˌtʃek 'aʊt/
coastline *n* /'kəʊstˌlaɪn/
coral reef *n* /ˌkɒrəl 'riːf/
creation *n* /kri'eɪʃn/ ***
crunchy *adj* /'krʌntʃi/
crystal clear *adj* /ˌkrɪstl 'klɪə/
cubic metres *n* /ˌkjuːbɪk 'miːtəz/
demolish *v* /dɪ'mɒlɪʃ/ *
diver *n* /'daɪvə/
dust *n* /dʌst/ **
evidence *n* /'evɪdəns/ ***
expand *v* /ɪk'spænd/ ***
forecast *v* /'fɔːkɑːst/ *
fuel *n* /fjʊəl/ ***
gene *n* /dʒiːn/ **
gentle *adj* /'dʒentl/ **
go on sale *phrase* /ˌgəʊ ˌɒn 'seɪl/
health spa *n* /helθ ˌspɑː/
hydrogen *n* /'haɪdrədʒən/
light *n* /laɪt/ ***
luxury hotel *n* /ˌlʌkʃəri həʊ'tel/
mainland *n* /'meɪnlænd/
maximise *v* /'mæksɪˌmaɪz/
monitor *v* /'mɒnɪtə/ **
ocean *n* /'əʊʃn/ **
on top of *prep* /ˌɒn 'tɒp əv/
palm *n* /pɑːm/ **
paradise *n* /'pærədaɪs/ *
playground for the (super) rich *phrase*
/ˌpleɪgraʊnd fə ðə (ˌsuːpə) 'rɪtʃ/
romantic *adj* /rəʊ'mæntɪk/ **
sand *n* /sænd/ ***
secluded *adj* /sɪ'kluːdɪd/
self-cleaning *adj* /ˌself'kliːnɪŋ/
so much to see and do *phrase* /ˌsəʊ ˌmʌtʃ tə
ˌsiː ən 'duː/
space *n* /speɪs/ ***
sports facilities *n* /spɔːts fə'sɪlətiz/
suck *v* /sʌk/ **
sunset *n* /'sʌnˌset/ *
surface *n* /'sɜːfɪs/ ***
technically *adv* /'teknɪkli/ *
tropical *adj* /'trɒpɪkl/ **
turquoise *adj* /'tɜːkwɔɪz/
twinkling *adj* /'twɪŋklɪŋ/
underwater *adj* /ˌʌndə'wɔːtə/
unsafe *adj* /ʌn'seɪf/
vegetarian *n* /ˌvedʒə'teəriən/
villa *n* /'vɪlə/ *
wall *n* /wɔːl/ ***
watch out for *phrase* /wɒtʃ 'aʊt fə/
whatever you do *phrase* /wɒt'evə jə ˌduː/
while away *v* /waɪl ə'weɪ /
wonder of the world *phrase* /ˌwʌndə əv ðə
'wɜːld/

Unit 2

adrenalin junkie *n* /ə'drenəlɪn ˌdʒʌŋki/
beach bum *n* /'biːtʃ ˌbʌm/
bed-and-breakfast *n* /ˌbedən'brekfəst/
blackened *adj* /'blæk(ə)nd/
bungee jumping *n* /'bʌndʒi ˌdʒʌmpɪŋ/
burning *adj* /'bɜːnɪŋ/ **
bustling *adj* /'bʌslɪŋ/
childhood *n* /'tʃaɪldˌhʊd/ **
cloudless *adj* /'klaʊdləs/
cluttered *adj* /'klʌtəd/
culture vulture *n* /'kʌltʃə ˌvʌltʃə/
curiosity *n* /ˌkjʊəri'ɒsəti/ *
dread *n* /dred/
excitement *n* /ɪk'saɪtmənt/ **
frosty *adj* /'frɒsti/
grapevine *n* /'greɪpvaɪn/

Unit 3

(one)-storey *adj* /('wʌn)ˌstɔːri/
actually *adv* /'æktʃuəli/ ***
architecture *n* /'ɑːkɪˌtektʃə/ **
art scene *n* /ɑːt ˌsiːn/
back streets *n* /'bæk ˌstriːts/
balcony overlooking the sea *phrase*
/ˌbælkəni ˌəʊvəˌlʊkɪŋ ðə 'siː/
barbecue *n* /'bɑːbɪˌkjuː/
big garden *n* /ˌbɪg 'gɑːdn/
brick *n* /brɪk/ **
bungalow *n* /'bʌŋgəˌləʊ/ *
buzz *v* /bʌz/
chalet *n* /'ʃæleɪ/
city that never sleeps *phrase* /ˌsɪti ðət ˌnevə
'sliːps/
cosmopolitan *adj* /ˌkɒzmə'pɒlɪtən/
cost of living *phrase* /ˌkɒst əv 'lɪvɪŋ/
cottage *n* /'kɒtɪdʒ/ **
crime levels *n* /kraɪm ˌlevlz/
Don't get (me) started *phrase* /ˌdəʊnt ˌget
(ˌmiː) 'stɑːtɪd/
funky *adj* /'fʌŋki/
get around *v* /ˌget ə'raʊnd/
haggle *v* /'hægl/
homesick *adj* /'həʊmˌsɪk/
I see what you mean *phrase* /ˌaɪ ˌsiː ˌwɒt jə
'miːn/
it's essential to *phrase* /ɪts ɪ'senʃl tə/
modern *adj* /'mɒd(ə)n/ ***
nightlife *n* /'naɪtlaɪf/
optimistic *adj* /ˌɒptɪ'mɪstɪk/ **
profession *n* /prə'feʃn/ ***
really *adv* /'rɪəli/ ***
relocate *v* /ˌriː'ləʊkeɪt/
remedial masseur *n* /rɪˌmiːdiəl mæ'sɜː/
roses round the door *phrase* /ˌrəʊzɪz ˌraʊnd
ðə 'dɔː/
set up *v* /ˌset 'ʌp/
shop till you drop *phrase* /ˌʃɒp tɪl jə 'drɒp/
soak up the history *phrase* /ˌsəʊk ʌp ðə
'hɪst(ə)ri/
stone *n* /stəʊn/ ***
stroll *v* /strəʊl/ *
swimming pool *n* /'swɪmɪŋ ˌpuːl/
take a risk *phrase* /ˌteɪk ə 'rɪsk/
that sounds wonderful *phrase* /ðæt saʊndz
'wʌndəfl/
that's great *phrase* /ˌðæts 'greɪt/
thatched roof *n* /ˌθætʃt 'ruːf/
the hustle and bustle *n* /ðə ˌhʌsl ən 'bʌsl/
the small hours *phrase* /ðə 'smɔːl ˌaʊəz/
thriving *adj* /'θraɪvɪŋ/
veranda *n* /və'rændə/
vibrant *adj* /'vaɪbrənt/
wooden *adj* /'wʊdn/ ***
wooden shutters *n* /ˌwʊdn 'ʃʌtəz/

Unit 4

absolutely *adv* /ˌæbsə'luːtli/ ***
boiling *adj* /'bɔɪlɪŋ/ *
bows and arrows *n* /ˌbəʊz ən 'ærəʊz/
brave *v* /breɪv/
brilliant *adj* /'brɪljənt/ ***
camel *n* /'kæml/
caravan *n* /'kærəˌvæn/ **
carry on *v* /ˌkæri 'ɒn/
climate *n* /'klaɪmət/ **
come across *v* /ˌkʌm ə'krɒs/
countless *adj* /'kaʊntləs/ *
crocodile *n* /'krɒkəˌdaɪl/
delicious *adj* /dɪ'lɪʃəs/ *
deserted *adj* /dɪ'zɜːtɪd/
dust storm *n* /dʌst ˌstɔːm/
endure *v* /ɪn'djʊə/ *
exotic *adj* /ɪg'zɒtɪk/
explorer *n* /ɪk'splɔːrə/
fabulous *adj* /'fæbjʊləs/ *
freezing *adj* /'friːzɪŋ/ *
gigantic *adj* /dʒaɪ'gæntɪk/
give up *v* /ˌgɪv 'ʌp/
head off *v* /ˌhed 'ɒf/
in the shade *phrase* /ˌɪn ðə 'ʃeɪd/
insomnia *n* /ɪn'sɒmniə/
kayaking *n* /'kaɪækɪŋ/
keep up with *v* /ˌkiːp 'ʌp wɪð/
midnight sun *n* /ˌmɪdnaɪt 'sʌn/
minuscule *adj* /'mɪnɪˌskjuːl/
mosquito *n* /mɒ'skiːtəʊ/
nomad *n* /'nəʊˌmæd/
nostril(s) *n* /'nɒstrəl(z)/
observatory *n* /əb'zɜːvətri/
ordeal *n* /ɔː'diːl/
packed (with) *adj* /pækt (wɪð)/
percentage *n* /pə'sentɪdʒ/ **
put up with *v* /ˌpʊt 'ʌp wɪð/
reputation *n* /ˌrepjʊ'teɪʃn/ ***
rock-bottom *adj* /ˌrɒk'bɒtəm/
seal hunt *n* /'siːl ˌhʌnt/
sky-high *adj* /ˌskaɪ'haɪ/
suffer *v* /'sʌfə/ ***
survive *v* /sə'vaɪv/ ***
tough *adj* /tʌf/ ***
trekking *n* /'trekɪŋ/
tribe *n* /traɪb/ **
tropical *adj* /'trɒpɪkl/ **
underground *adv* /ˌʌndə'graʊnd/ *

Unit 2 (continued)

hilly *adj* /'hɪli/
inn *n* /ɪn/ *
landmark *n* /'lændmɑːk/
leafless *adj* /'liːfləs/
look in every way *phrase* /ˌlʊk ɪn 'evri ˌweɪ/
misty *adj* /'mɪsti/
moonless *adj* /'muːnləs/
overpowering *adj* /ˌəʊvə'paʊərɪŋ/
paragliding *n* /'pærəˌglaɪdɪŋ/
paved *adj* /'peɪvd/
rent a cottage *phrase* /ˌrent ə 'kɒtɪdʒ/
rocky *adj* /'rɒki/ *
source *n* /sɔːs/ ***
sunbathing *n* /'sʌnˌbeɪðɪŋ/
surrounded *adj* /sə'raʊndɪd/
take pictures *phrase* /ˌteɪk 'pɪktʃəz/
toasty *adj* /'təʊsti/
travel light *phrase* /ˌtrævl 'laɪt/
travels *n* /'trævlz/
trip of a lifetime *phrase* /ˌtrɪp əv ə 'laɪftaɪm/
twisting *adj* /'twɪstɪŋ/
winding *adj* /'waɪndɪŋ/
zone *n* /zəʊn/ **

Communication activities

Student A

Unit 1, Language study Ex 5 page 67

Report the information in the newspaper extracts to student B. Then ask student B to guess which fact
is true.

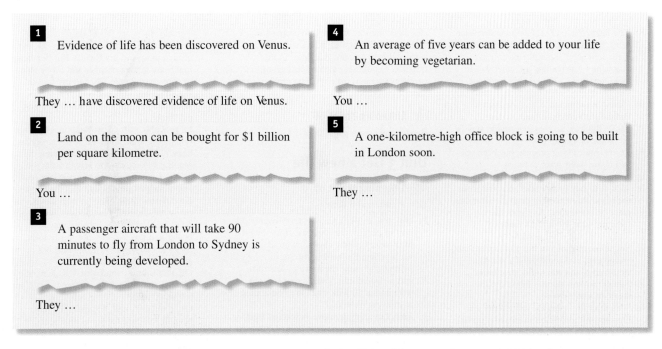

1

Evidence of life has been discovered on Venus.

They … have discovered evidence of life on Venus.

2

Land on the moon can be bought for $1 billion
per square kilometre.

You …

3

A passenger aircraft that will take 90
minutes to fly from London to Sydney is
currently being developed.

They …

4

An average of five years can be added to your life
by becoming vegetarian.

You …

5

A one-kilometre-high office block is going to be built
in London soon.

They …

(Sentence 3 is true. The scramjet, which uses hydrogen as fuel, will be able to travel at over 8,000 km/h
and will technically be flying in space. It is forecast to carry its first passengers in 2025.)

Listening scripts

Unit 1 Life's a beach

Listening script 01

(P = Petra; R = Ray)

P: Hi, Ray. Back from some exotic location?

R: No, no – I'm working nearer home at the moment.

P: I thought of you the other day. You worked on that island in Dubai, didn't you?

R: The Palm? Yeah – I was doing underwater work there for about six months actually.

P: Well, there were some photos of it in a magazine I was reading the other day. It looks amazing … but how on earth did they do it? And what exactly is it made of?

R: I know, it's difficult to imagine, isn't it? Basically, it's made of sand.

P: Sand? But how do they get sand to stay in the shape of a palm tree?

R: Er, it's quite a long process, but I can tell you if you really want to know.

P: Yes, I really am interested.

R: Well, first they bring rocks and sand from the mainland, then they drop the sand into place on the seabed. As I said, that's basically what the island's made of.

P: They must use a lot of sand.

R: Yes, apparently, if you put all the materials end to end, you could build a wall that would go round the world three times.

P: Blimey. So how do they get it into the shape of a palm tree?

R: Well, after dropping the sand in the sea, they spray it into place and build it up to the surface to make an island.

P: Oh, I see. But how do they stop the sand moving?

R: They put this covering on top of the sand – it's made of some special material called 'geotextile' – and then they put rocks on top of that.

P: Right. So what exactly were you doing?

R: Well, they use divers to check that everything is in the right position and that's what I was doing.

P: Ah – I bet you earned a fortune.

R: Yeah, the pay was good, but I still wouldn't be able to afford a place on the island. They've designed the Palm as a kind of playground for the super rich. I think about 5,000 people can live there and there are luxury hotels, theme parks, restaurants, shops, health spas and loads of sports facilities.

P: Wow, it sounds like paradise.

R: Yeah – it's been described as the eighth wonder of the world.

P: You're kidding! And is it true that you can see it from space?

R: That's what they say.

Listening script 02

Reading text from page 68

Listening script 03

Reading text from page 69

Unit 2 The open road

Listening script 04

Reading text from page 70

Listening script 05

I woke up on a boiling hot morning in India and looked out of the window of my room at beautiful trees swaying in the breeze and a cloudless blue sky. Where I was staying was a three-star hotel situated near a river. It was surrounded by ancient buildings. In the distance, I could see several small groups of people washing in the river. The predominant smell was spices.

Listening script 06

Reading text from page 73

Unit 3 Get a new life

Listening script 07

(P = Presenter; J = Jem)

P: Welcome to *Get a new life*. Over twenty per cent of people who emigrate from the UK to another country choose Australia. Today we have Jem Pickford in the studio – he's planning to make the move to Australia and we asked him how his preparations were going. So Jem, when are you hoping to move to Australia?

J: Erm, I'm going to move as soon as I get my visa and that can take up to 12 months.

P: Oh, really? That's longer than I thought. So what are you doing in the meantime?

J: Well, I'm flying over to Australia next week just for three weeks to look at locations of where I'd like to live. It'll probably be on the north side of Sydney. I'll be staying with my brother and hopefully he'll have found some information for me.

P: And is that why you chose Australia – to be close to your relatives?

J: Actually, there are several reasons. Er, the weather is a big one. Emotionally I'm very affected by climate, and British winters depress me. Then the other reason I'd like to move to Australia is that there are better work opportunities. I'm a remedial masseur and the Australians are becoming more and more health-conscious, so massage is getting very popular there.

P: Oh, that's great. Jem, you mention the weather – but you could have gone to the south of France, for example. Why Australia?

J: Well, the weather is one thing, but the main problem of moving to a country like France is the language barrier. In my profession it's essential to be able to communicate with my clients.

P: Oh yes, I see what you mean. OK, Jem, how different do you think your life will be in Australia?

J: Erm, I think the main difference for me will be to do with the climate. I'll be able to pursue my favourite sports virtually all the year round. I'll be able to swim and play tennis and I'll be near the sea so I'll be able to enjoy the beaches. Another difference is that I might be commuting to work on a ferry across Sydney Harbour instead of sitting in a traffic jam every morning.

P: What about your social life over there?

J: I think Australia is very similar to the UK. It might be a shock if I moved to a country area where they're really conservative, but I'm hoping to be very near Sydney. The social life there is more café-oriented because of the weather, but that's really nice.

P: You're not going to miss home at all, are you?

J: Actually, there are lots of things I'll miss about the UK. I think particularly the rest of my family and my friends. But hopefully flights are getting cheaper and I'll be able to come back to the UK and my friends will come and visit me.

P: What are you going to do when you first get there?

J: I'll probably start off working in a massage salon there and I think I'll rent a small flat, hopefully with a balcony overlooking the sea. But I don't want to stay in a flat too long – as soon as I've got myself settled, I'm hoping to get a house. But the houses are different there – they're bungalows, not two-storey houses. Traditionally, houses are only one-storey there because they're cooler and it gets pretty hot in summer. So I'll get a bungalow with a nice big garden and a barbecue.

P: Oh, that sounds wonderful. OK, Jem, one last question. Where do you see yourself in ten years' time?

J: Oh, gosh, erm, well, hopefully, I'll have been in Australia for about nine years by then and I'd like to think that I'll still be enjoying the things I enjoy now. In other words, I'll be going down to the beach regularly, I'll be playing tennis every day and I'll be swimming a lot. And with a bit of luck, I'll have set up my own practice, I'll still be working and I'll have found a nice place to live.

P: Well Jem, good luck. Please let us know how it goes. And comments from you the listeners please on the radio message board.

Listening script 08

Language study Ex 5 from page 76

Listening script 09

Reading text from page 77

Listening script 10

OK, tonight on *Get me out of here!*, one of you lucky people is going to win a house and a chance to start a new life in one of these places. They are:

One
With a huge population plus millions of annual visitors, Hong Kong Island is a seriously vibrant place. Get ready to shop till you drop. Hong Kong for the visitor is all about shopping – back streets full of action, sounds and colours. Temple Street Market is a must for evening shopping – don't be afraid to haggle. Or, visit a fortune-teller to have a face and palm reading. The city has thousands of sit-down restaurants. The local dishes start from about £1 and the service is really quick.

Two

Since the wall came down in 1989, Berlin has re-defined itself as Europe's coolest capital city. The number of hotel beds has doubled and tourism is doing a roaring trade, attracting those in search of a more unusual city break. It's a massive city, four times the size of Paris. Berlin is a really funky city and most of that funk can be found in the eastern side. Berlin is also renowned for its thriving art scene. Nightlife in Berlin doesn't kick in until after eleven. A popular pre-club venue is the Strand Bar in the area called Mitte where they've tried to recreate a beach party feel. They've even got their own sand.

Three

Buenos Aires is one of the world's biggest, liveliest, up-all-night capitals. It's a city that never sleeps. Getting around is easy – taxis are a bargain and $2 gets you to most parts of the city. La Boca is in the historic port district. The Football Stadium is located here – football being the lifeblood of this cosmopolitan city – and it's the practice ground for the Boca Juniors. Free tours around the stadium are available – check out the seats reserved for famous footballer Diego Maradona.

 Listening script 11

Welcome back to *Get me out of here!* OK, contestants, are you ready? The rules are very simple – you will hear three questions, each one to be answered with a number. The closest answer wins. Good luck, everybody. Let's start with question one: Hong Kong returned to China in 1997 after how many years of British rule? Question two: how far, in kilometres, is Berlin from Paris? And finally, question three: what's the population of Buenos Aires? Remember, the closest answer wins …

 Listening script 12

And now the moment of truth. How did you do? Here are the answers. One: Hong Kong returned to China in 1997 after one hundred and fifty years of British rule. That's one hundred and fifty. Two: Berlin is eight hundred and seventy-seven kilometres from Paris. Eight hundred and seventy-seven. And finally, three: the population of Buenos Aires is three million. Three million. And we have a winner. The winner is …

Unit 4 Going to extremes

 Listening script 13

Reading text from page 79

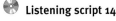 **Listening script 14**

1 Erin

Can you imagine living in a place four times colder than your freezer? That's what it's like here. After a few minutes outside in freezing temperatures of minus 50, your nostrils fill with ice and you can't wiggle your toes. Everybody wears furs and you need at least two pairs of trousers with tights underneath. And if your nose turns white, you need to get inside fast. In winter the streets are deserted, but it can get pretty boring being cooped up indoors for days. A lot of babies are born in autumn! But there's somewhere even colder than here. In Oimyakon, about an hour by plane from here, temperatures reach rock-bottom – it can get as cold as minus 70.

2 Jamie

Just to give you an idea of how crowded it is here, the population is seven times denser than in Manhattan – New York is nowhere near as crowded as this place. And the worst thing about it is that, not only is it a concrete jungle, but rents are sky-high too – a small three-room flat can cost as much as $8,000 a month. Our bedroom is so small the double bed touches the wall on three sides.

3 Lisa

It's like walking into an oven here – it's boiling even in the shade. People try to escape the heat by getting up early and not doing too much in the afternoons, but outside the town, people still do everything by hand, even in temperatures like these. It regularly gets up to 50 degrees Celsius. What surprised me to begin with was the clothes people wear – you'd think that people would walk around wearing barely any clothes at all, but actually in extreme heat like this you have to avoid dehydration. So people tend to wear layers of cotton robes to keep the moisture in and act as insulation.

4 Arturo

The last time it rained in Atacama was in 1971 and that was the first time for 400 years. The best thing about Atacama is that it has by far the purest air in the world, and this means you get amazing views of the stars at night. In fact, they're building a gigantic observatory on top of a mountain here. But of course we need water to live here. There are some oases where you can get water underground but that only accounts for a minuscule percentage of the water we need. It has to be piped in from outside.

5 Halldora

In summer, we have daylight for more than 20 hours a day and it really brings out the party spirit – the streets are packed with people dancing all through the night. They call Reykjavik 'the Ibiza of the north'. From mid-May to mid-July nights are as bright as days, and after the dark winters people go crazy. It can be so bright at three in the morning you need sunglasses. My daughters used to wake early, but I never put special blinds on the windows – only foreigners do that. It's simply the most wonderful time and we all try to enjoy it. I sleep at least one-and-a-half hours less in the summer. I can catch up on my sleep in November, or when I'm old.

 Listening script 15

Pronunciation and speaking Ex 1 from page 81

Unit 5 Review

 Listening script 16

(P = Presenter; T = Tom)

P: Welcome back to *Home is where the heart is* and with me is London-based musician Tom Kenny. Tom, who plays guitar with up-and-coming pop band, The Change, is a true London aficionado. He first came to London several years ago and since then has lived all over the city. Tom, first question, where do you live and why?

T: Now I live in Covent Garden, which is a really happening part of the city. The first time I went there I was immediately struck by how vibrant it was. I've been there for about three years now. I've been to other parts of London to look at other houses, but I always get back thinking, 'Thank goodness I'm home.'

P: What's your favourite place in London?

T: Trafalgar Square. I like the fact that whenever anything good happens, it's like, 'Let's all go down to Trafalgar Square.' It's great to see it packed with people and to be part of it. You really feel like you're in the heart of London.

P: And your least favourite?

T: The new Wembley Stadium. I suppose it looks OK, but it really is soulless. The old stadium had such character and such an amazing history.

P: What's your idea of a perfect Friday night?

T: Something completely unplanned. London is the best city in the world for nightlife. I love the hustle and bustle of the West End and on Friday nights it's really buzzing, so I suppose I'd head there and then see what happens. The West End has loads of funky little back-street clubs that have live music – so we'd probably end up seeing a band at some point.

P: Where would you want to be taken on a date?

T: I'd like to be taken for a walk around London. It's one of the most romantic things you can do – just wandering around soaking up the atmosphere. I love it when it's late and the streets are totally deserted. And maybe we'd take a late-night trip on the London Eye and watch the city lights twinkling away below us – as long as there was no-one else up there with us, of course.

P: What's the first piece of advice you'd give to a tourist?

T: Whatever you do, make sure you check out the British Museum. It's a really cool place to while away a couple of hours or so. They've got lots of interesting stuff there.

P: Well, on that note, I'll say thanks to Tom for telling us why his heart is in London. Next week, I'll be joined by journalist and writer Leila Davis, who'll be talking to us about …

 Listening script 17

Song from page 84

Communication activities

Student B

Unit 1, Language study Ex 5 page 67

Report the information in the newspaper extracts to student A. Then ask student A to guess which fact is true.

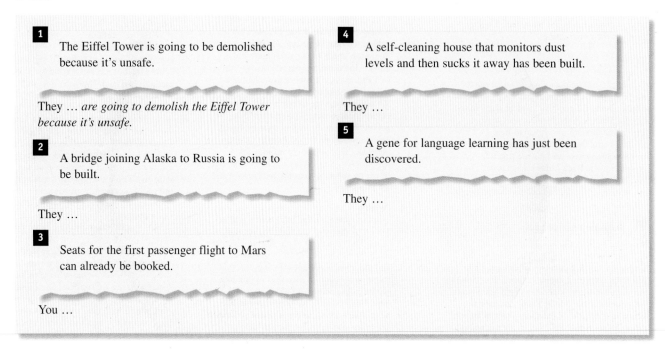

1 The Eiffel Tower is going to be demolished because it's unsafe.

They … *are going to demolish the Eiffel Tower because it's unsafe.*

2 A bridge joining Alaska to Russia is going to be built.

They …

3 Seats for the first passenger flight to Mars can already be booked.

You …

4 A self-cleaning house that monitors dust levels and then sucks it away has been built.

They …

5 A gene for language learning has just been discovered.

They …

(Sentence 4 is true. Sensors monitor the levels of dust in the atmosphere and then calculate how much will have settled on the room's surfaces. A huge extractor fan then automatically sucks away the dust.)

Extra practice, Unit 1 Ex 4 page 86

1 85
2 1 million
3 1995
4 2002
5 2,000
6 600 billion billion